HOLDING HANDS
WITH
GOD

HOLDING HANDS
WITH
GOD

*Catholic Women
Share Their Stories of
Courage and Hope*

Sexual Abuse

Hopelessness

Divorce

Child's Death

Widowhood

Miscarriage

RONDA CHERVIN

Our Sunday Visitor Publishing Division
Our Sunday Visitor, Inc.
Huntington, Indiana 46750

Our Sunday Visitor Publishing Division
Our Sunday Visitor, Inc.
200 Noll Plaza
Huntington, IN 46750

ISBN: 0-87973-577-5
LCCCN: 97-67056

Cover Design by Monica Watts

Printed in the United States of America
577

To all women who need to find the Love of Jesus: Savior in the midst of terrible pain and anguish.

Table of Contents

Introduction

Why Holding Hands With God?

For twenty years I have been giving lectures and workshops about Christian women's concerns. Always there are some participants who leave dissatisfied. They tell me, "Ronda, what you said was good, but it didn't go deep enough into problems like mine."

Sometimes these difficulties involve pain I myself have experienced, such as the suicide of a child, or a mastectomy. Then I can not only empathize but also witness to the ways I found Christ in the very dreadfulness of that agony. But many times the problem is one I've not had, such as sexual abuse, alcoholism, or extreme overeating. Yet, I have met other women who did come through such trauma and now live in hope.

Finally, I thought of a remedy. Why not get the survivors to write their stories for other women still experiencing nearly unbearable darkness?

I have been greatly moved by reading the accounts I have assembled in this book. My prayer is that you may find comfort and light from God as well.

— Ronda Chervin

Ronda Chervin is a widow, mother, and grandmother. She is a speaker for the Speakers Bureau of Franciscan University of Steubenville. She has been a professor of philosophy and theology at Loyola Marymount University, Notre Dame Apostolic Institute of Arlington, Virginia, St. John's Seminary of the Archdiocese of Los Angeles, and the Franciscan University of Steubenville. The author of some forty-five books concerning Catholic life, Ronda is presently a member of a religious community called the Handmaids of Nazareth.

Chapter One

Betty Mitten

You Are Special:
Abused Human Dignity

Ronda: Many women grow up with a negative attitude about themselves, that they are never good enough, smart enough, pretty enough, thin enough. They see themselves as inferior — inferior to others in their circle of friends, their peers, their teachers or supervisors, and even inferior to their own brothers and sisters. Why? Where did they obtain this notion of inferiority? Why do they cling to it? How does it affect their lives and their relationships? What can heal them of this? In this sharing, Betty Mitten will present a witness and teaching helpful to women with many different reasons for feeling unhappy about themselves.

You! Yes, you! Did you think I was talking about someone else? Did you turn your head thinking someone else must be there? Why don't you think you are special? Has no one ever told you so? Well, then, let me tell you: You *are* special. Why? How? Let me count the ways . . .

- you have been made in the image and likeness of God;
- you are a unique human person;
- you have value just because you are.

In today's world, we tend to equate someone's worth or value with what they do, what they contribute to the economy (or subtract from it!), or how they make the world a better place. How much money did you earn last year? How many trees did you save? What innovative contribution have you made? While these things may have relative importance, nothing compares to the idea that you *are*, you have been individually made and have worth, not so much for what you can *do*, but for who you *are*. You have dignity because you are a human person.

Do you doubt this? Do you feel worthless, a burden to people? Have others told you that you are no good? That you never do anything right? Do you have a constant negative view of yourself? These thoughts are not uncommon to those who have had their human dignity abused.

While many things are being said about child abuse or the physical abuse of spouses, little has been presented to address the issue of abuse to human dignity. This abuse may not include physical abuse. On the contrary, it is often accompanied by no physical contact at all — the nurturing hugs of a mother and/or father, the essential recognition of self-worth, even status as a member of the family. Perhaps the child was not even desired by her parents. Perhaps she often felt ignored, unappreciated, and unloved.

In addition to the lack of physical contact, dignity abuse is often the result of bitter and critical words. These words are said without thought, especially without consideration of their detrimental effects. The words focus on the negative, the things that you, the individual, are not: not good, not pretty, not smart, not a boy. They may point to achievements that you have not made: you can't do that, you never do anything right, you'll never amount to anything.

These words cut to the heart! After hearing these over and over again, is it any wonder that you begin to believe that they must be right? I *am* no good. Everyone does things better than me. I should have been a boy!

Parental abuse affects the individual's relationships within

11

the family. There may be a distance between siblings, a lack of interaction because of feelings of inadequacy. Suspicions of favoritism may be raised, or an older sibling may copy the abuse of a parent and demoralize a younger sibling. The abused child may be very shy and a loner, and though desperately in need of love, may erect walls to hide assumed deficiencies and prevent further hurt. Unwilling to risk hurt in order to affirm others, she may grow cold from preoccupation with self.

Yet because those who are abused are in great need of love and affirmation, they often allow themselves to be treated like slaves. In this way, they think they will find the love they seek. They will do anything in order to please the one who will never be pleased. In speaking about her relationships with the other sisters in her convent, Blessed Faustina says, "I learned that certain people have a special gift for vexing others. They try you as best they can. The poor soul that falls into their hands can do nothing right; her best efforts are maliciously criticized" (*Divine Mercy in My Soul, The Diary of Sister M. Faustina Kowalska*, Marian Press, 1987).

This criticism influences the abused person in such a way as to affect her outlook on herself and those around her. Abused people believe themselves to be inferior to others. They strive for perfection but never reach it. Even if they attain a perfect score, they are not satisfied with what they have done. Some never see their work as leading to success so they settle for second best or even worse, just don't try at all because they feel destined to fail.

Abused people often end up in co-dependent relationships. The need to be needed leads them to take on boyfriends, lovers, spouses, and even bosses who continue the abuse. They cling to those they hope will give them value, and yet if they place no value in themselves, their lover or boss will have none for them either.

The abused are prone to addictions as well. They seek affirmation in things they think they can control. They may be workaholics, exercise fanatics, or eccentric housekeepers. They constantly compare themselves to others. Body shapes, hair styles, clothes, height, shape of lips: everyone else's is always better. And then who can compare with the women on the cover of the magazines that are at the checkout aisle of the grocery store? The result may be eating disorders as the abused seeks to find satisfaction in food or in the rejection of food. Those who long for escape may find it in drugs or alcohol.

Unfortunately, the abused may become the abuser. Repressed anger may flare up out of control, resulting in violence toward others. The anger may be directed against those in compromising situations, for example children, elderly parents (especially when these are the perpetrators of the initial abuse), even clients or customers. The (often unconscious) attitude is: "I'm not respected so why should I respect you?" Women whose dignity has been abused may abuse their own bodies because their bodies have little or no value to them. They search for love in promiscuous sexual affairs, yet feel empty and rejected when morning comes and the bed is empty again.

How do those who have had their human dignity abused break away? Is there anything that will lift them from the abyss of nothingness and bring them into the light of hope? One of the first steps is to be aware of the problem. This may be the first time that you have seen the issue addressed, or taken time to read something like this. Perhaps you are just becoming aware of this situation in your life. Why has it taken so long? Am I really that stupid?

No, you are not. You may not have recognized the situation as abnormal because you've never known anything else. For you, abuse has been the norm. Likely, your relationships have reinforced the negative. Even the close friends you've made probably have had similar experiences, which may be why you feel comfortable with them. They don't expect much from themselves, nor do they expect much from you.

Acknowledging the abuse is very painful. It is like touching an open wound. The pain may be so intense that it is easier to ignore the abuse, pretend it didn't happen or really is not that important. You're not in the abusive situation anymore so it doesn't matter; your life is not affected by it. Or is it? What patterns of behavior described above can you identified in your life today? Are these behaviors destructive to you and your relationships with others — your spouse, your children, your friends and co-workers? Healing requires the wound be opened up and cleaned out. This process is painful but necessary for proper healing. And that is the goal: to be healed.

So what is this human dignity that has been abused? Can I retrieve it? Am I really a unique individual created in the image and likeness of God? What does this mean? What is this "being" that I'm supposed to be?

Genesis tells us that God created man as male and female, in His image and likeness (Gn 1:26-27). He blessed them and found everything that He made to be good (Gn 1:28, 31). Being in God's image means that we have a rational soul, one that thinks, reasons, and freely chooses. These attributes are inherent in our being. We are "somebody," and this sets us apart from everything else in the visible world.

We are made up of a body and soul that are inseparably intertwined. Perhaps we can define a person as a rational soul, incarnate in a fleshly body. We are not a person without our soul nor are we a person without our bodies. Our souls communicate through our bodies. Yet we are incommunicable, that is, we are so complex that we can never be fully comprehended, at least not by another human being.

God knows us intimately. He alone can fulfill our deepest needs. His love is unconditional and unending. The true dignity of a person is derived from his/her union with God. This union has the power to transform, to raise us to be the person God has made us to be. We are blessed, and we are good! Our value does not depend on how others perceive us or upon our accomplishments. Our worth is not based on our earthly doings but on how we are seen in the Father's eyes. To him, we are human beings, not human doings! And we are precious in his eyes!

A major step in the healing process, and perhaps the hardest, is showing mercy. We must forgive those who have been the abusers. But first, we must honestly identify who they are. Maybe we are quick to blame one person when perhaps there was a second or third person who also shares in this blame. Perhaps we rationalize why one person has caused the abuse (perhaps he or she was abused), and yet there is another person who has also contributed to the hurt still felt. An objective look is difficult but necessary.

Another person in need of forgiveness from you is you. An abused person stores a lot of self-guilt. You may feel, from years of constant reminders, that you have brought all this upon yourself. If you weren't so worthless, people would not tell you that you are. Plus, you live with the effects of abuses that you have chosen — with your attitude toward those around you, with the addictions, with the unhealthy or immoral life choices. You live with the knowledge that whatever happens to your body happens to your soul, and try as we may to see them as separate, they are not. If your body is abused, so is your soul.

But you sense the hope. You want to break free of addictive habits and bad life choices and heal your wounded human dignity. To do this, you must be willing to love — not only others but yourself as well. The opposite of abuse is acceptance.

People must return to the perception of love as a virtue, not just an emotion. As John Paul II advises: "Only a person can love and only a person can be loved. . . . The person must be loved, since love alone corresponds to what the person is" (*On the Dignity and Vocation of Women*, no. 29). The will of the one who loves must be oriented to the value of the one loved. John Paul II says that a woman wants to love so that she can show love; she can only find herself by giving love to others. Yet a woman is only capable of making herself a gift if she believes in her value as a person and in the value of the man to whom she gives herself. In *Love and Responsibility*, John Paul II says "A love . . . is itself real love only when it reaches the highest point of affirmation of the dignity both of its object and of the subject itself."

Love is a full self-giving. Only in a sincere gift of self can a

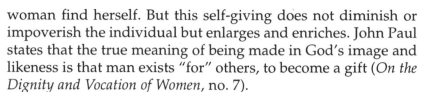

woman find herself. But this self-giving does not diminish or impoverish the individual but enlarges and enriches. John Paul states that the true meaning of being made in God's image and likeness is that man exists "for" others, to become a gift (*On the Dignity and Vocation of Women*, no. 7).

Through love, the dignity of a woman shines forth. Saint Augustine says that the dignity of a woman is measured by the order of love. She must be free within herself, allowing her freedom and courage to come forth. She must be able to exercise her intellectual and creative faculties without a submissive dependence on others. In this way, a woman regains her strength. Learn to be secure in saying no to burdensome and unfruitful work. See yourself as serving in ways that are life-giving to others and to yourself. Pursue service in a role that is suitable to you and to your talents and gifts. Realize this is wise, not selfish. When we are in the right role, we can freely love.

There is cause for rejoicing here. In freedom, we appropriate God's choice to create us. With joy we acknowledge this divine act. In freedom we joyfully obey God and accept our responsibility for our relationship with God and with others. We have a freedom to obey in love and faith.

We are all, while living, in the process of growth. We do not need to be fixed in unhealthy patterns but must reach for the help of God and pull ourselves into the Light, the Light of Christ. As Pope John Paul II tells us in *On the Dignity and Vocation of Women*: It is Christ who knows the dignity of each one of us, our true worth in the Father's eyes.

Betty Mitten is a medical technologist with an M.A. in Theology and Christian Ministry from Franciscan University of Steubenville. She is the head house mother at a residence for pregnant women and an aspirant for a Carmelite monastery in Santa Fe, New Mexico.

Chapter Two

Ronda Chervin and Theo Stearns

Will I Ever Feel Good Again?
Hopelessness

Ronda: A year or two ago I was visiting one of my favorite women friends, Theo. It happened we were both feeling rather down and gray — not in total despair, but still sad and miserable enough to set aside more cheerful topics and try to brainstorm how we thought God would want us to get through such times in a better way. Here is the result for you to ponder.

"I guess this is what people call depression. I have no motivation to do anything at all. I drag myself out of bed to get my children ready for school, then lie in bed and stare at the ceiling, wondering if I'll have the strength to face the rest of the day."

"Since my husband died, I've lost all desire to continue my life. I wish God had taken us together in that fatal accident. I still work and people think I'm doing very well, but I keep hoping another drunk driver will finish me off."

"It's been ten years since I had an abortion. I was in my teens and everything seemed to add up to getting rid of the 'unwanted pregnancy.' I was not a practicing Catholic and I didn't feel guilty about it, but after the birth of my first child I felt worse and worse. I went to confession, but I am riddled with guilt and think that God can never forgive me for murdering my baby."

Hopelessness has many faces. It could be near despair over failure to overcome sinful addictions, or chronic rage. It may be anxiety about present financial or personal difficulties, or terrible memories of the past.

When emotional states are intense, hopelessness seems justified. In our feelings of worthlessness we can become convinced that we are damned. Out of our desperation we may put the blame on others for causing our sinful behavior. Hopelessness becomes a force in itself, leading to fears of insanity or suicide. Whatever face it takes, hopelessness leaves feelings of anguish and futility, a sense of being alone in the dark.

Patterns of behavior that are associated with hopelessness include withdrawal from family, friends, God or the Church; inability to cope with the tasks of daily life; and viewing others as the cause of our problems. These harmful patterns can be broken when we understand the meaning of darkness in our lives and the healing power of Christ and his Church.

Scripture never claims that life will be all sunshine and roses, nor does it describe the path to holiness as one victorious climb to the top of the mountain. In fact, we are told that the way is rough and narrow (Mt 7:14), that we must walk it bearing a cross (Mt 16:24), and that our journey must be undertaken with fear and trembling (Phil 2:12).

Jesus himself endured agonies of helplessness and rejection in trying to win us, his beloved children, to accept him. Jesus willed to endure human suffering with his infinite intensity for thirty-three years — not to spare us all suffering but to give us ultimate victory over it, and in the end eternal happiness.

Hopelessness actually grows from false ideas about the way life should be. Our own ideas about how we make the journey to heaven can become obstacles to hope. The most basic of these false ideas can be called "the utopian mind-set": An attitude that perfection — whether physical, intellectual, moral, or spiritual — can be achieved in this life and thus make us feel secure and happy. For modern women, this utopian mind-set expresses itself in the images of perfection presented to us by the media: the sleek, aerobic body, a mind sharp as a knife, and a heart sweet as sugar. As Christian women, we pursue the ideal of perfect marriage and family life or perfect service to God in religious or single life. Rather than movie stars, we choose saints on which to model our lives. Yet even with good intentions and holy examples, we find we cannot attain perfection.

When we encounter our own human weaknesses and failures, when we discover that we are not as patient as Saint Monica or as sacrificial as Saint Clare, we become disappointed and frustrated. Yet the saints, too, had their struggles, failures, sins and, yes, even feelings like our own. Saint Thérèse, the Little Flower, seems so sweet and elevated on a holy card, but this same little saint suffered depression, grief over loss of loved ones, painful illness, and great spiritual darkness.

Although we are called to admire and imitate the saints in their devotion, we cannot expect to model our lives directly after theirs. After all, we each have our unique crosses to carry and obstacles to overcome. Problems arise when we think that reciting one more Rosary or taking a more submissive attitude will lift us above the struggle; rather, such spiritual practices should give us light and courage to face the struggle and even make the difficult changes necessary to alleviate some of our depression. Someone dealing with guilt from a past abortion may not find that the contemplative response of Mary Magdalene will ease the pain. It might be more healthy emotionally and spiritually to engage in active pro-life work.

Depression over marital problems can arise if one chooses to simply offer up the sufferings in silent resignation, instead of confronting the long-term patterns of unforgiveness and anger that demand attention.

False utopianism declares that we have no right to be sad, that we can always find one more way to cope, and that we shouldn't be a burden to others. This refusal to admit weakness and to open ourselves to others is based on the false idea that the perfect Christian can deal with her own problems and doesn't need anyone else. This is not spiritual perfection or humility but a form of pride, a rugged individualism which is contrary to the Holy Spirit.

What, then, is the true meaning of darkness in our lives as revealed by God? The Christian ideal is not being an island unto oneself but is rather loving God with our whole heart and our neighbor as ourselves. To reach out to God and neighbor requires a sense of utter dependence on God and an admission of our frailty. It is only in acknowledging our weakness that we can have compassion for our neighbors and their failings.

Feelings of depression are often allowed by God during transition periods in life, as part of what the doctors of the Church call "the dark night of the soul." To be purified from arrogance, complacency, harsh judgment of others, and the numerous evils we don't even see in ourselves (though most of our friends see them every day), we have to hit bottom.

We try to escape these "dark nights." We often feel so ashamed of our inability to cope that instead of admitting our weakness and meditating on our need for purification, we find ourselves incapable of even talking about our hopelessness. When the tension is relieved and the hopelessness seems to have passed, we try to forget about it, to leave it behind as fast as possible. Instead of learning from our woundedness which brings healing, we cover it up so the wounds fester, only to erupt again under stress.

Although it is natural to want to avoid pain, it is not good to run away from the trials God sends for our purification.

Sometimes we think we can find a quick insight or spiritual lesson to shorten the process; but nothing can substitute for the experience of enduring the pain, of reaching out to God as Jesus did during the agony in the Garden. If it was the will of the Father that Jesus, the God-man, would save us, not by a blazing word of truth but only through excruciating humiliation, can we imagine that our holiness could be bought at a cheaper price?

In the hell of hopelessness, depression, guilt, or loss, all is dark. Just as husband and wife, without turning on the light, can reach for each other at night and feel comforted, so in faith we can cry out to God and grab his hand tight enough to feel just enough strength to go one more hour, depressed but still able to get out of bed, guilty but still able to go to the sacrament of Reconciliation for forgiveness, grieved but still able to love.

At the peak of our natural powers, we think we can do great things: raise a perfect family, save the Church from dissent and laxity, renew our religious order.

At times of hopelessness, when we so acutely experience our human weakness, we have to be satisfied and grateful for anything we are able to accomplish with God's grace.

These experiences of depression can actually be turned to great spiritual good. At these moments, we lean completely on the Lord, for there is no one else to turn to. When confronted with emotions and situations we cannot understand or deal with, we must go to Jesus and say, as the disciples did, "To whom shall we go? You have the words of eternal life" (Jn 6:68).

Once we acknowledge our need for the Lord and, by an act of sheer will, trust in his grace, we will find it easier to cope. The old gospel song, "One Day at a Time," becomes our anthem. In fact, we may be reduced to operating one hour at a time. We may feel like the scrubwoman who is faced with a huge tile floor to clean: The entire surface seems overwhelming, but to scrub one tile at a time is manageable.

Besides seeking God's grace moment by moment, we need to use our God-given common sense. We should watch for patterns in our depression: Is it related to our menstrual cycle? The monthly hormonal changes that occur in women often bring on bouts of depression. It's a relief to know that the hopelessness we experience may be a result of physiological factors and will soon pass or can be treated. A visit to a doctor to check out other possible causes for depression may be helpful.

Living one step at a time may seem inadequate in our fast-paced society, but often it is the only way those struggling with hopelessness can overcome. To reach out to God and to reach out to our neighbor is the path to healing; it may take a while, but every little step brings us nearer the light and out of the darkness.

Here are some small steps — little deeds of love — that we can accomplish:

• Start each day with a morning offering. Here is one: Oh Jesus, through the Immaculate Heart of Mary, I offer you my prayers and works, joys and sufferings of this day in union with the Holy Sacrifice of the Mass.

• Go to Holy Mass daily if possible and to the sacrament of Reconciliation once a month.

• Pray throughout the day, *even if you don't feel like it*, such as reciting the Hail Mary or just repeating, "Jesus, help me!"

• Be happy with small accomplishments such as cleanup of one room, or preparing one class, finishing one desk job, writing one letter to the editor, or calling a sick friend.

• Find activities at home or at work which involve the least amount of pressure.

• Find a friend who is a good listener; talking about our problems helps reduce stress.

• If depression is affecting your work situation, talk it over with a supervisor. Honest discussion might relieve the workload during this trying time.

• Exercise each day, if only for ten minutes.

• Reach out to someone else who needs help; taking the focus off your own troubles helps break the bonds of depression.

Sometimes the first step is the hardest: To admit that we need help. Yet in taking that first step, great healing may begin. There are many sources for help. Consider support groups and twelve-step programs for addictions.* There are grief groups and even more specific groups such as Women Exploited by Abortion. No experience of hopelessness is so unique that it can't be helped by the Christian love of other sufferers.

Get information on professional psychological counseling. Ask for direction through your priest or other pastoral counselors in your parish. You may wish God would save you alone, privately, but he may want you to receive healing partly through his Church.

Hopelessness comes from the fear that evil will triumph over good in our lives. We can be reassured by the words of Pope John Paul II, "The power of Christ's Cross and Resurrection is greater than any evil which man could or should fear" (*Crossing the Threshold of Hope*, 219).

When confronted with hopelessness, we can echo the words of the Holy Father: "Be not afraid!"

*An excellent series in magazine form and also on audio tapes of a Christian version of the Twelve Steps can be ordered by writing to Father Emmerich Vogt, O.P., The Twelve Steps Review, 375 NE Clackamas Street, Portland, OR 97232-1198.

Theo Stevens is a member of the Third Order Dominican Community of St. Martin de Porres, holds an M.A. in Catechetics from Notre Dame Apostolic Institute of Arlington, Virginia, and is a mother and grandmother.

Chapter Three

Natalie A. Nelson

"Arise my love, my fair one, and come . . .": Eating Disorders

Ronda: In our culture where being thin and glamorous is so stressed, being heavy or even slightly overweight can be the source of painful darkness. Programs of diet and/or Overeater's Anonymous can be helpful, but many women need to combine physical, psychological, and spiritual approaches. Natalie Nelson's witness story provides fresh insights that may help all readers concerning a positive self-image as a daughter of God.

"Lead, Kindly Light, amid the encircling gloom
—Lead Thou me on!
The night is dark, and I am far from home
— Lead Thou me on!
Keep Thou my feet; I do not ask to see the distant scene — one step enough for me.
I was not ever thus, nor pray'd that Thou shouldst lead me on.

I loved to choose and see my path, but now
— Lead Thou me on!
I loved the garnish day, and, in spite of fears, pride
ruled my will: remember not the past years.
So long Thy power hath blest me, sure it still will
lead me on,
O'er moon and fen, o'er crag and torrent, till the
night is gone;
And with the morn those angel faces smile
Which I have loved long since, and lost awhile."
— *John Henry Cardinal Newman*

One day in December, 1991, I looked in the mirror and realized that I had gained about thirty pounds. I had been attending UC Santa Cruz for three months, and somewhere in the middle of the partying and depression, I had unwittingly realized one of my biggest fears — being overweight. Panic set in, and I learned what it meant to be utterly disgusted with oneself.

Since then, I have struggled with losing the weight, but I have also struggled with trying to recreate my conception of myself as a beautiful, beloved daughter of my Lord in the process.

I presuppose that those who would be personally interested in this topic are those who have felt, or at least wondered if, they are experiencing the potential insanity of dealing with a weight issue, specifically the problem of overeating. I am increasingly aware that overeating is extremely common today among women — especially young women — and that it permeates even the holy minds and hearts of strong Christians. Many girls come to me seeking help, admitting their powerlessness under this oppressor.

The obsessive person thinks and rethinks the obsession constantly. Add compulsive behavior — the acting out of a mental obsession — to the obsession and the combination may lead to, as in my case, a sort of insanity. I experienced the terror, guilt, frustration, and hopeless despair that I would never be well again.

Having been involved in Alcoholics Anonymous for four and one half years, I knew that *eating* was not the problem; *I* was. The overeating is but a symptom of the sickness of my unhealthy mind and spirit. But I know, too, that I am a daughter of God who created me in his divine image; and so I ask, what is the source for this foggy vision that causes me to see myself as an ugly duckling and consequently treat myself as such?

There are a number of reasons why a woman becomes an overeater (anorexic, bulimic, and so on). Most of the time, the reason dwells in one or more past experiences in which the individual has been hurt and her self-worth distorted. Some examples of painful and wounding experiences include:

• sexual abuse (it has been said that eighty percent of women with eating disorders have undergone some form of sexual abuse);
• having [an] alcoholic parent[s];
• abandonment by parent[s] or family member[s];
• overly rigid, uncaring and emotionally negligent parent[s];
• being raised in a society which promotes immodesty, promiscuity — the exploitation of women.

Essentially, any experience that taints your vision of yourself and wounds you can give rise to an eating disorder.

In addition to the food addiction, any one of these same reasons may also lead to the development of negative feminine traits. A woman's self-dignity may be destroyed, causing her to see herself as a mere material body. This attitude leads to a sort of Gnostic view in which a woman grows to hate her body because it has become soulless, simply a thing on display or at the disposal of others for visual or physical pleasure. Ironically, this can also lead to an emphasis on the body and its features even more. She may become vain and seductive, seeking pleasure in luring others to herself because her body has become her sole source of self-esteem. She may become spiteful and complaining, taking out on others the contempt she feels for herself or she may grow domineering or aggressive. She may internalizing her lack of control with eating by trying to control others, or may try to get attention by becoming oversensitive and whiny. She often feels like the victim of an attacker.

As these negative traits escalate in frequency and intensity, so too does the compulsive behavior. She makes endless attempts to stop herself; and then she continually abuses herself for failed endeavors. Her self-esteem drops even lower and she feels locked in. The vicious cycle is drowning her, and she knows utter despair. The panic sets in because she realizes she is a *slave!* She feels completely hopeless. Nothing she has done or is doing has stopped or even significantly lessened the obsessive/ compulsive behavior. Despair.

Most overeaters, for reasons yet obscure, have lost the power of choice in eating. Our so-called willpower is practically non-existent. At certain times, we are unable to bring into our consciousness with sufficient force the memory of the suffering and humiliation of even a week or month ago. We are without defense against the first binge.

This is the point at which healing must begin. The primary and most crucial element of healing is surrender. Your back is against the wall; surrendering to God is the only and saving option. In the Twelve Steps of Alcoholics Anonymous, the Third Step is this surrender, turning our will and our lives over to God. As Catholic women, we know him to be our Lord and Savior Jesus Christ, and to him we turn it over. We need to relinquish all attempts at control over our lives and let God be the master of all. We must drop in humility to our knees and lay it all — the feelings, the pain, the ideals of "fixing" the problem, the failed attempts, the panic and despair, even the excitement of a "successful" day — at the feet of our personal, and infinitely loving, best friend and redeemer, Jesus. We can do nothing! But he can do all, in his merciful omnipotence.

Sometimes, though, you may feel as if you *are* speaking

words of surrender over and over again, and nothing is getting any better. You are still plagued by the obsession and compulsion and continue to fall flat on your face. What you're doing isn't working! You are exactly right. What you're doing is *not* working, nor will it ever. You can't do *anything*, remember? God does and will do it all. In fact, you can't even *surrender* by yourself! You need to either visually, or actually, lie prostrate before the Lord and ask him to help you surrender. The Twelve Steps suggest this prayer:

"My God, I offer myself to Thee, to build with me and to do with me as Thou wilt. Relieve me of the bondage of self [and sin], that I may better do Thy will. Take away my difficulties, that victory over them may bear witness to those I would help of Thy Power, Thy Love, and Thy Way of life. May I do Thy will always!"

This prayer cuts to the quick and points out that you are the problem, but by offering yourself to God, he can make you an instrument of his peace. Now I say this prayer constantly throughout the day, and I am reminded always of who I am — an overeater — and of my utterly dependent place in this world.

Along with the surrender necessarily must come acceptance. You need to accept that you have an eating disorder and that you are powerless over it; furthermore, you must also accept the world around you — on *its* terms, not yours. As women, we need only to fine-tune ourselves to the positive tendency in our natures to trust. In trusting God, we can attain this peaceful acceptance of the world in which we live.

Total acceptance of yourself and your situation cannot happen unless you confront your past. This means different things for different people. Those with deep wounds may need to seek professional counseling. Others may, on their own, be able to remember the experiences and examine them, perhaps writing these and the accompanying feelings in a journal or on paper (which can be burned later as part of the "letting-go" process), or by telling an entrusted person and then taking them to God in prayer.

This will likely be a very difficult process, especially if you have tried your whole life to do the opposite — bury the painful past. This is very difficult for women because once locked into a negative cycle with the associated negative traits, we tend to be passive. Add diminished self-esteem and what happens is that we don't feel worthy to take up the world's time with our problems, or we greatly fear others' reactions to our shameful past. But you must be brave! Allow God to console you, his beloved child.

A crucial fact that must be recognized when hoping for — expecting — healing is that "healing" does not *remove* the past. Your experiences will not magically vanish from your recollection, nor will God extract them from your memory. Furthermore, those times will probably never be remembered by you as anything but unpleasant (at the very least). The scar they have made upon you is permanent. But the wound can be healed! Sometimes this happens in a single beautiful moment in which you just feel thoroughly washed clean by Jesus' precious blood, and the memories cease to be poignantly painful. But for many of us, the healing takes place over several years or more. God slowly penetrates our hearts and minds with his soothing light and gently heals the sores. Only after much healing has taken place do you realize what he has been doing all along.

The point here is not to dwell on the times you have been hurt but to confront them and try to accept their presence in the tapestry of your experience. Be open to having God — on his time, and working as he often does through others — touch you with his healing grace.

We pocket our pride and go to the pain, illuminating every twist of character, every dark cranny of the past. Once we have taken this step, withholding nothing, we are delighted. We can look the world in the eye. We can be alone at perfect peace and ease. Our fears fall from us. We feel the nearness of our creator.

This reflection leads to perhaps the most fundamental and necessary aspects of healing — prayer and reception of the sacraments. This cannot be emphasized enough! If you run in and out of Mass once a week, or even for a minute of prayer daily, what time are you giving God to work in your soul? Jesus is a personal God, with whom we have, or are working toward having, a loving *relationship*. Relationships involve spending time with the beloved. You need to put in the time. Remember, nothing *you* do alone will cure your sickness, but what you *do* have to do is give God the time. There are times when you feel you are doing well. "Maybe I can skip Mass today." But where did you get the grace to do so well the past few days? Surely it wasn't a new solution you thought up. God nourishes us by his own precious body and blood. He gives us the spiritual food necessary to live sanely and serenely. Never underestimate our need and dependence on him. Just sit for a second and remember where you came from — utter despair. Still thinking about skipping prayer time or Mass for something "more important"?

The final element in the healing process is often neglected. Discipline is frequently overlooked because it is associated with willpower which you know you don't have, and yet you need to be disciplined.

Before you jump in with "There's no way! I need to accept that I am powerless over food," have you ever asked yourself [in prayer] what areas of your life lack discipline? Do it. Sometimes, we obsess so much because we have the time to do so. Our daily lives are very sloppy, without schedules or routines. Many people see this as carefree living. Maybe. But those of us who are sick need order. Would you invite a guest into a messy house? Likewise, while God will enter a soul which is messy, distracted, and unfocused, you won't find him because you are not fully receptive. When your daily life is in order, you naturally put more direct energy into every single task. Discipline is crucial to a fuller day-to-day existence.

Discipline is not perfectionism. Remember *progress, not perfection*. Behind perfectionism lies a hidden fear that others will not approve of you as an imperfect person. But we can *never* be perfect! The human condition is one of trial and error. By our very natures as creation, we know this to be true. By retaining the mind-set of the perfectionist, you set yourself up for failure in all your endeavors. This is inevitable.

While perfection is a tortuous ideal, growth is not. The obsessed person needs to focus on positive actions — tell yourself what *to* do. The word "don't" does not register in your brain. If you tell yourself, "Don't eat that piece of cake, or that second piece of pizza," the "don't" doesn't sink in. What will register is "Eat that piece of cake, or that second piece of pizza."

See every single moment as a new one. Realize that you are only controlled by the past, even the previous moment, insofar as you allow yourself to be. Don't beat yourself up if you falter. With God, you can start fresh any second.

"For lo the winter is past, the rain is over and gone. The flowers appear on the earth; the time of singing has come, and the voice of the turtledove is heard in our land. The fig tree puts forth its figs, and the vines are in blossom; they give forth fragrance. Arise, my love, my fair one, and come away" (Sg 2:11-13). Remember, with the sacrament of Reconciliation, you are a truly clean soul.

What about the obsessive thoughts that plague you every day, even at the waking and sleeping hours? Replace them with thoughts and words of truth. While feigned solutions have consistently failed you and the messages that you are ugly have aided in your destruction, truth will never harm or fail you. Rather than giving in to words of self-abuse, learn words and prayers of encouragement and affirmation to speak to yourself. For example, for women who are so enveloped in vanity:

"Let not yours be the outward adorning with braiding of hair, decoration of gold, and wearing of robes, but let it be the hidden person of the heart with the imperishable jewel of a gentle and quiet spirit, which in God's sight is very precious" (1 Pt 3:3-4).

Do not strive to be feminine. Rather, strive to be holy, and in becoming more of the creature God intended you to be, your femininity and beauty will radiate naturally and brilliantly from your being.

You must remember that your body is a temple of the Holy Spirit. It truly is a walking tabernacle. Meditate on that, and then treat your body as such. Be healthy. Give your body what it requires to be the most fit and proper receiver of our Lord, and to be physically what it was meant to be.

Pray to Mary. Establish a relationship with her. She should be our model, especially of the vital virtues of modesty, purity, and chastity. These virtues are seldom mentioned today, let alone mentioned as ones desirable for women. These virtues will transform your sense of dignity and worth as a woman, and Mary can and will teach them to you. All women are to be revered *as* women.

Finally, make efforts to see the beauty and goodness of all God's creation. In other people, in nature, in music — you will find and taste the sublime beauty of God's very self. He gives us so much! See it and love it as he does.

Some practical actions to take on a *daily* basis are needed for you to jump into the process. Here are a few suggestions:

• Make gratitude lists. Every day, remember, and write down all that God has done for you. This helps you get out of the negative messages that ever encroach upon your mind and spirit.

• Make examinations of conscience. Also, daily recollect and write down all the times throughout the day your thoughts, words, and deeds did not reflect Christ. Ask the Holy Spirit to show you where and when your heart is not like Christ's.

• Personal prayer and reception of the sacraments. Daily! Morning, noon and night.

• Be of service. Serve God through his creation. And do it joyfully! Even a smile, to someone who is sad, can bring Christ to an immortal soul, and in so doing, serve the master who made and loves you.

The more you build your life with Christ, the more he will put your life in order and relieve you of your "unhealth." He loves you infinitely and wants his beloved child to be happy and forever smiling. He will take away your crosses if you let him, so that you may better serve him in his earthly kingdom! Something to let roll off your tongue:

"God, grant me the serenity to accept the things I cannot change; courage to change the things I can; and wisdom to know the difference — living one day at a time; enjoying one moment at a time; accepting hardships as the pathway to peace; taking, as he did, this sinful world as it is, not as I would have it: Trusting that he will make all things right if I surrender to his will; that I may be reasonably happy in this life and supremely happy with him forever in the next. Amen."

Natalie A. Nelson is a theology student at Franciscan University of Steubenville.

Chapter Four

Jane Hamilton

Locking Arms:
A Fiancé's Cancer

Ronda: I was talking about the concept of this book with an editor. She said, "I have a friend with such a great story for you." Here it is.

I phoned James when I got home from an interminable grammar seminar. "Happy February second! I love you. Happy second anniversary. I wish our schools weren't in two different cities. How was work?"

I wound my finger into the cord as I sat behind stacks of assignment sheets, handouts, and graded papers — the walls of a fort.

"Something's wrong," I said, "and if you tell me it's nothing, I'm hanging up on you."

Then my boyfriend told he'd discovered a lump on his body.

We got engaged on February third, after the doctors decided James had testicular cancer.

We all have an ideal self we'd like to pull out of our photograph albums to show the world. "That's how I behave in a crisis," we'd announce, and then we could sign autographs and answer questions as the Woman Who Has It All Together. We are heroes racing into the burning building to save the trapped infant; we are dark-suited agents flinging their bodies before the President to protect his office.

February third. I sat on the arm of the desk chair. At some point, James started crying on the other end of the phone, in Ithaca (New York) at about 2:15 a.m.

"What do they want to do?" I said.

"Operate," he said. "Tomorrow. I can't come to Brockport (New York) then."

James and I think differently during crises. James freezes. After his doctor said "cancer," James says he heard nothing else. He gripped himself so he would stay in control during the taxi ride to his third-floor, college-student apartment. As for me, an Iron Jane snapped into place, glass armor standing between the world and me. The emotions washed against it, and I watched.

"I can come to Ithaca," I said.

Alone, James had no idea what to do first, so I gave him a list. He'd been unable to come from Kansas when his grandfather died, and his family had arrived during the last days of his grandmother's illness. He'd never dealt with doctors enough to see the pomposity of a doctor melt once the patient and his family inform themselves of their options. No one had shown him how to handle mortality. I had seen it all — in the illness, suffering and death of my grandmother.

I have to take control in a crisis. My instinct makes me grab the telephone. While James took the list I'd given him and checked off each completed task, I got on the phone with three professors, the Catholic community, a friend from InterVarsity Christian fellowship, and my mother. I say stupid things in shock.

"I wanted you to know," I told my Mom, "that I'll be in Ithaca this weekend, because I didn't want you to worry in case you called and I wasn't at home because James is having his right testicle removed because he has cancer."

My mother gave me a list of things to do, proving some

tendencies are hereditary. While I got the prayer chain started, she phoned every friend of the family involved in the medical profession. My stepfather's friend Mariana, a doctor in Michigan, telephoned James late that night and convinced him an immediate operation was the best choice.

I called James back and told him that when he spoke to Father Murphy, he had to tell him we'd gotten engaged so that he could get the six-month waiting-period clock running with the Church. We had intended to get married after graduation. With time at a premium, the engagement became official.

For me, then, the flurry of activity ended. After James assured me he didn't want me driving icy roads in the dark, I found myself stuck in Brockport until the sun rose. Sitting at my desk, surveying the windblown snow, I thought: "We're supposed to pray when we're in trouble." So I tried. Staring at the carefully shoveled sidewalk, I opened up my heart the way I always had before, but this time: "God — you b#^%*&!."

I snapped tight, frightened at the anger, frightened because I'd never felt any of that before. Job's wife, I realized. If you touch me I don't care, but harm someone I love and I'll lash out. We blame Job's wife for condemning God, but it's a very female response, a community-oriented answer to pain within our inner circles.

James had calmed by eleven that night. Father Murphy had climbed three flights of stairs despite his arthritis to give James Communion and anointing of the sick. James felt easier, and we made plans to meet in time to get him to the hospital the next day.

February fourth, 6:00 a.m., after saturating my body with caffeine, I headed for Ithaca.

The day in the hospital passed in twenty-four hours, like every other day. It didn't get longer because of its importance, nor did it shorten because I wanted it to end.

I met efficient doctors, caring nurses, a man in the waiting room who told me fish stories ("It was *this* big!") and a volunteer who talked to me about graduate school and gave me her recipe for risotto before smuggling me into the recovery room to brush the hair from James' eyes as he awoke from anesthesia.

"My head's full of cotton," he told me, pale as he lay on the stretcher in his white hospital gown beneath two white hospital blankets.

I asked the nurses about stitches (internal), follow up visits (next week), and symptoms to monitor (fever, bleeding, nausea). I called his parents and mine. I got his medication.

When we got home well after nine that evening, I bought two slices of pizza for dinner — James had said he wouldn't want any, but the aroma roused him enough for half a slice. I spread my sleeping bag on the floor and sat watching him. We prayed together before shutting off the lights. "Help me understand," I said.

No one should get married before enduring one crisis and one ten-hour car trip: so says my mother. People's true personalities emerge when circumstances destroy careful plans and invalidate our assumptions. It's true not only in marital relationships. Sincere friends mobilize during an emergency, gathering close to ward off the blows. In crisis, we gravitate toward the people we trust, even if they're not our best friends. I had friends I didn't trust in the crisis; not fair-weather so much as fragile. I told one of my housemates about the operation before I left. The others I would tell on my return, and only if they asked.

James had felt isolated in Ithaca after my graduation the previous June, but that week he discovered the quantity and caliber of his friends. Friends visited us after his operation, bringing board games or just to have dinner.

The Catholic community rallied around him, and around me. I went to daily Mass whenever James felt well enough for me to go, and the priests gave me the Eucharist for James. I prayed for him with a chill inside, though: how to ask the God we felt had abandoned us to return to the fix the problems he'd allowed to happen? If God hadn't protected James, where was the certitude? Did it benefit us to believe?

The primary community grew between James and myself. I wanted to marry right away if the doctors predicted he'd live only a year or less. We didn't know yet what kind of cancer he had. Nonseminomas kill a man in months. The tumor had been huge, and seminomas grow slowly. We learned new words: teratocarcinoma, orchiectomy, infarction. We had ten days before the lab returned a decision, and we spent them in quiet tension.

Four days after his operation, James phoned some friends. From the next room I heard him talking about me, how strong I had been for him, how I had done his shopping, how I'd encamped in his living room to cook for him and take care of the apartment. He didn't tell them how I swept the whole kitchen in a fit of anger because he wouldn't talk to me, or that I'd broken down on his shoulder one night after the visitors departed.

He didn't know I'd cried in the hospital while he slept, trying to put words into my journal and discovering they'd abandoned me too.

February ninth. After five days in Ithaca, I changed worlds again. Back in Brockport — an oral report on Dickens' *Bleak House* due in three days when my own life seemed so much bleaker. While trying to read *Arcadia*, my mind wandered to Ithaca, to February fourth, to Room 413 in Tomkins County Hospital.

In the end, I did give my oral report. I did read my assignments. I completed the papers. I automatically showed up at work and tutored students who complained about not owning cars and not vacationing in Jamaica. I agreed to be a bridesmaid in my friend Teresa's wedding. I cooked and cleaned. I calculated my income tax. I sang in choir every Sunday. The glass armor had settled so closely over my soul that I couldn't see it any longer. I moved through every day as though checking off items on a list of things to do.

Back in Ithaca, people James had considered casual friends from his gaming group had planned a spontaneous movie night for the day after I returned to Brockport. He "telecommuted" to work, accessing the larger machines from home, working on digital analysis problems I could barely pronounce, let alone understand. LAPACK, which he said *as ellaypack*, and ULLV. He could talk at me about LAPACK for half an hour, but he forgot to tell me when the doctor phoned a test result, got silent when I asked about further treatment. I read him Renaissance poetry after my class covered it, and I met the same listening silence I devoted to LAPACK.

February twelfth. The labs decided James had grown a seminoma after all, meaning we faced a two-part decision. Did James want to have radiation therapy, if so, where?

First he went to the doctor on his student health care plan, a gentleman who had to wait a week to look up the answer to every question, including, "How many treatments will I get?"

When I voiced my disgust, a fellow graduate student recommended his brother's doctor, a radiation oncologist at Sloan-Kettering Memorial Hospital, the best cancer hospital on the East Coast and arguably the best in the world. My mother fronted the four hundred dollars for an initial visit, only fifteen dollars of which insurance covered. (So much for managed health care.)

The doctors gave the same verdict — seminoma is mild enough that it rarely spreads, so we wouldn't think of remission. Without any therapy, James had an 85 percent chance the cancer had not spread; in other words, he might be cured already. If he underwent radiation therapy, that possibility climbed to 99.7 percent. The New York doctor's professional manner impressed James so much more than Doctor "I'll-have-to-look-that-up," that James considered living with my mother for the month of therapy.

James and I have different standards. James used every excuse to delay the decision, and he concentrated on money. Sloan-Kettering would charge sixteen thousand dollars for the treatment, money James didn't have. I never considered money an issue since I would have emptied my bank account and taken out loans to get the best treatment possible, and both my father and my mother had offered James substantial sums. James showed a resentment I hadn't expected: He didn't want to rely on other people. Insurance only covered the "allowable" outside Ithaca, and judging from past performance, might "allow" ten dollars a treatment.

Aside from money, communication became a source of contention. James would get test results from his doctors and not tell me, or he would go through long periods of time without a call or e-mail. I didn't get a letter from mid-February until April. I would phone every other day, ask questions repeatedly, prompt him to tell me how he felt or what he wanted.

The stress spilled over. I sat through more than one grammar lecture writing in my journal, fingers pressing the stress-induced pain over my heart, hiding the tears that escaped, trying to stop thinking about pills or a jump from the window.

I didn't tell James about those times — he had other worries. The treatment might sterilize him. We debated banking sperm — we prayed and consulted others; I even called a sperm bank before we opted against it. James and I prayed together afterward, but even then he couldn't say how he feared I'd leave if staying meant I couldn't have the brood of children in our daydreams.

We learned our different styles can cause explosions: James withdrew from me when the waiting became difficult. He felt my family pressured him to rush, while I felt he procrastinated because he feared decisions. James refused to question the doctors on any detail, while my mother and I refused to believe anything they said.

My daydreams darkened. In early mornings at my job — a tutor without students to tutor yet — I sat wishing I were dead. I didn't want to kill myself, or to die: I just wanted to be dead. As James grew quieter and called less often, I tightened, my soul corkscrewing as I worked harder and more intensely on every assignment. I began to forget appointments, and I grew silent in crowds. I attended meetings as if watching them on television. When on February twenty-third I couldn't get death off my mind, I e-mailed two friends at Cornell, and one e-mailed back to me; the other called me that night. They phoned James and made him call me, but the daydreams persisted: darkness, stillness, silence, sleep.

February twenty-eighth: James had resumed work in his office, using that as his excuse for not phoning the doctors to press them for information. He said he was busy. "Too busy to worry about your health?" I asked. It was the Monday after the bleak Wednesday. "Don't you understand the pressure to get this done?"

James lost control then, the words exploding from his diaphragm. "The only pressure I feel — is from you and your mother to have me make every decision instantaneously!"

I froze, said nothing for more than five minutes, long-distance rates. Too many thoughts came too quickly — I stared into the headlights of the disaster, no idea what to do first. Shock.

I had done everything I could, and I didn't have anything left inside, not motivation or purpose or energy. It couldn't only have been a hundred annoying acts of mine that caused it. He'd grown this anger for weeks and lashed out at the doctors and fate by hitting an easier mark. But I didn't have words, not even to react. I could picture his standing with one leg propped up on his desk chair. At some point, I didn't know when, I had begun crying on the other end of the phone from him, a hundred fifteen miles away from Ithaca, New York.

I stretched out on the carpet, my face on my arms, the phone cradled near my ear in case he said something. He didn't. I tried not to breathe near the phone. I let tears run into the thirsty fabric of my blue sweater. Nothing. For minutes.

"I can't," I said. I couldn't breathe right — I had to inhale every three words and speak slowly. "I can't do this. I tried my best, but I can't. There's nothing left."

James sounded small. "I'm sorry."

But I couldn't recover myself. I drowned the phone, sat with my knees up and my spine into the wall. James hesitantly apologized once more. Somehow I said I'd call back.

After I hung up, I moved in a silent sea. I'd never known total stillness. The Iron Jane. I let the glass armor hold my spirit in place where it had broken. *I need to get ready for bed*, I thought, and I brushed my teeth and changed into pajamas. I didn't cry. I took my time. I folded the backlog of clothing piled on the desk chair. I straightened the sheets on the bed. And then: *I don't have to call him back. I can walk away forever.*

I did call. The panic and loss returned the instant I spoke to him, as though the glass armor could only hold in isolation. He apologized, and I apologized. I'd put pressure on him because indecision has always caused me more anxiety than a known difficulty. He'd procrastinated because the choice frightened him, and he had forgotten this choice involved two of us. He promised to talk to me more frequently. I promised not to pressure him. But during the next week I broke down in tears four or five times, more often than I had during the whole bout with cancer. Also, during that week, James chose Sloan-Kettering.

Early March. InterVarsity still prayed for James regularly, and every time I went to a meeting or a Bible study, four of five members stood a little too close and asked about him. They continued offering assistance: If I needed to leave town quickly they could talk to my professors, my boss, my landlord. My friend Teresa, a nutritionist who had gotten engaged the same week we did, sent James pamphlets about diet during radiation therapy. I continued to sing on Sundays for Brockport's Catholic Community, and the chaplains took care of me, being gentle when they spoke, repeating always that God let this happen for a purpose. I still felt God had done it deliberately. God has put out his hand and grasped James' life just to show me he could do it.

I learned that the Internet can become a family. As the crisis pulled me further from my house mates, I dialed into the network more frequently. The chatter gave a sense of community — virtual friends when the flesh-and-blood variety had withdrawn to social lives and schoolwork.

Later March, early April. Life isn't ever easy, I told myself, and I told it to others, and I told it to James. James began and completed radiation therapy, living with my mother in New York City for a month. I spent spring break accompanying him on the subway to the hospital, making sure he took his medicine to counteract the nausea of radiation sickness. I arranged for James' mother to stay for two weeks when I couldn't be in New York, and I helped arrange for his aunt to visit as well.

I surprised James with a visit for Easter weekend; the nausea and weakness had sent him to bed early, but I heard him get up in the middle of the night, and I sat on the stairs. When he saw me, he blinked a few times, then said, "Oh, sweetheart."

He held me for a long time in total quiet because everyone else had fallen asleep. He kept repeating, "You're here." The weekend passed, and I returned to school. I sent cards as often as I could, knowing he'd appreciate the reminders of his extended community in both Brockport and Ithaca. And I survived.

"It's tough for you," Teresa said to me, and I replied, "I'm fine." I'd phone James and say, "It's tough for you," and he'd assure me he was fine as well. After a month of radiation sickness, nausea, subways, and phone calls, the treatments ended. Cured. James returned to Ithaca. My mother sent a card telling me how well we'd dealt with the crisis.

Summer came — time to return to NYC to work on the novel I meant for my Master's thesis. I had initiated the project in April, but after those last weeks of class, finals, and the last stress pain in my heart, the book died. Pen in hand, I sat trying to write more than a paragraph at once. I read, and I worked on old projects, but the new one held no attraction. I spent hot June afternoons flat on my bed, sweaty but unwilling to turn on the air conditioner. I never felt hungry. I didn't play the radio.

While I lingered over the New York newspaper in the morning, in Ithaca, James went to work on his Ph.D. He played with Space-Time Adaptive Processing while both "space" and "time" lost their meaning for me, who had adapted so well to the responsibilities, who had flattened down and clung during the ripping winds of February and March. I tried to write about the experience, but I couldn't "process" it. I moved like a ghost over the weeks, walked through hours without leaving footprints.

It took until July to feel hungry again. Teresa's friends collaborated to buy a wedding gift, and I felt able to help arrange the project. I contacted old friends, the first time in six months. I went to daily Mass, praying without requesting anything in particular. Maybe God listened; maybe I couldn't hear him any longer. I worked on my novel, a hundred pages in the first three weeks of August. I spent time alone still, but I didn't struggle under the malaise. I took up jogging and cheered the first time I ran a full mile.

In the last week of August, Teresa asked me and Mary, another bridesmaid, to write the general intercessions for her wedding ceremony. We sat down, Mary and I, trying to come up with meaningful ways to pray for a newly married couple. "For Teresa and Ted," I began, "that the commitment they have made before God will strengthen them to live through the struggles and joys of marriage, we pray to the Lord."

Mary thought of the next one. "For their parents, that they may delight in the love their children have found, we pray to the Lord."

Mary composed the next few: a prayer for friends, for travelers, for the future. I said, "And for all married couples, that the sanctity of their commitment to each other before God may extend from themselves into the larger community, we pray to the Lord."

Is that what I learned? I couldn't say then if James' illness had taught me only the gift of survival, or instead the peace of finding ourselves on the other side of chaos. Had I only put words together so they sounded good, or did I really believe Teresa's commitment to Ted, and mine to James, should inspire the world? Could it really repay the community for all the strength we had drawn from them during our weakest moments? When God had seemingly left us to drown, had he instead used us as an example of his strength and might? Or were my attempts at understanding just the howling wind of Job? Two years later, I am now married to a cancer-cured James. Sometimes the anger at God returns, but I hope that's a sign of recovery: Anger at God is still contact with him, and I try to work through each issue as it appears. I ran headlong into a face of God we try to keep away from in our ice-cream-and sprinkle-sermons, and like any relationship in the same position, it's changed because of that. My friends at InterVarsity distanced themselves when they sang about love and I laughed darkly. Love is a fire, holiness is steel, and grace is raw power: Each one devours the soul that encounters it.

I've imagined God as an author; since we are made in his likeness, then possibly we can understand aspects of God by studying aspects of ourselves. At times I force my characters to confront pain in order to learn something about themselves so they solve their story's central conflict. The ones I love most, suffer most. It is a hard love I have for them, but I love them for what they become. As an author, I suffer beside them.

Perhaps God aches with us here, as he pushes us into a becoming we don't want and cannot understand. Sometimes we just cling, blind with the hope that purpose exists somehow; raging into the wind doesn't help as much as locking arms with the person beside us and holding tight. When we're too scared to lock arms with God, we can lock arms with the community.

*Jane Hamilton is the pen name of a writer. Her novel **The Guardian** was published by Thomas Nelson.*

Chapter Five

Ronda Chervin and Judy Bratten

The Wounded Side of Christ: Mastectomy

Ronda: Most writers will agree that there is relief from pain in finding the words to describe a darkness into which light came unexpectedly. The piece to follow is a woman-to-woman dialogue between two of us who found a way to survive a trauma many woman suffer or fear to undergo.

Mastectomy: The word itself is traumatic to a woman. Removal of a breast to prevent the spread of cancer strikes at a woman's most basic feelings about herself and life. Cancer threatens her existence, her plans and hopes, even her faith. Mastectomy threatens her femininity, her ability to nourish new life, and her self-image. Yet even this anguishing experience is an opportunity for God's grace.

We share here our personal journeys to grace through our mastectomies for those who have already had such surgery and those who fear it for themselves or loved ones.

Ronda's Story

It was a routine mammogram that gave me the first clue. As a strongly intuitive person, I was sure that I did not have cancer and that the tests were merely precautionary. Even when directed to have a biopsy — just in case I might be that one out of four women whose lumps are malignant — I was blithely convinced that I needed no treatment. My only acquaintance with mastectomy came from the witness of Ruth Guth, a dear holy friend. She described how her own horror over her surgery had been overcome when God sent her an image of the Infant Jesus being held close in the cavity where her breast had been removed.

My admiration for the spiritual manner in which my friend had confronted such trauma opened me to the possibility that if I were similarly afflicted, there would be some hidden grace for me.

Strange to myself, and stranger still to outsiders, when I learned that mastectomy would be the treatment of preference, my first response was humor! Funny phrases, such as "less is more," raced through my mind or sprang to my lips. Mary Betten Mitchell, who gives workshops on spirituality and humor, likes to tell her audiences to pick out the worst event of the day and try playing it for comedy rather than tragedy. Well then, humor could work for something as daunting as a cancer diagnosis.

Of course, most friends thought I was in a stage of denial. They reassured me that they wanted to be the ones to whom I could unburden my hidden, unbearable fears. I can well understand how terrible these would be in the case of a younger woman or a potential breast-feeding mother, but for a woman in her fifties married to a loving husband who insisted that surgery was the way to go, it didn't seem that I would have to fear the loss of a breast as the worst possible fate.

I was to discover, however, that my loving Savior had something better in store for me than humor and resignation. During the ten days between the decision and the actual mastectomy, I was praying alone in a church after my daily Communion, looking up as usual at the large crucifix hanging behind the altar, when Jesus fixed my gaze on his wounded side. Familiar images from the devotion to the Sacred Heart began to pass through my thoughts: "Hide me in your wounds," "The Church flowed through the wounded side of Christ." Suddenly I realized: *After my mastectomy, my side will look like the wounded side of Christ!*

How glorious! I always pray that I may imitate Christ. I have read with wonder and awe the accounts of the martyrs, so thrilled to resemble their beloved Lord by being crucified like him. The holy stigmatics have always attracted me by the depth of their spiritual union with Christ, a union so poignantly accompanied by physical signs.

In an instant, the future ugly scar that was to disfigure me as a woman became instead a visible sign of grace. "I belong to my beloved, and he belongs to me."

I know that some women want to keep their breast surgeries private. In spite of the options of plastic surgery and prosthesis, who wants to be stared at with pity for years afterwards? In my case, being a seminary professor surrounded by prayerful brothers and sisters, I was sure that it would be better for me to announce my surgery beforehand so that all could pray for a good outcome, followed by a rapid recovery and the strength to continue my work.

Out in the world, one might think of concealing one's cancer for fear of being fired, but I received only expressions of concern, care and offerings of special Masses and prayers from priests and sisters all over the country.

Accustomed to relying on "earning love" through good works, I found it a great interior healing to receive so much tenderness simply because I was weak and needy. I think it is because of this *inner healing* that now, after the surgery, friends say I actually look better than before.

While recuperating from the mastectomy, during which time I was surrounded by my loving husband and friends, I received another spiritual insight. It has been revealed to us that during the Crucifixion, the Sacred Heart was consoled by the love he would receive throughout the future ages from his true followers. I could now understand this mystery better, for it seemed almost worth the physical pain to receive so much love.

My spiritual guides suggested that since the seminary is the "womb of the Church," it was right that, as part of the formation faculty, I should be pierced with a sword as was Mother Mary. With her, I offer all the pain of this time for our future priests.

Nonetheless, I was a bit afraid as I prepared to look down at my scar for the first time.

Now, I thought, *it will come: the horror and the grief.* There was some of that. Read the following poem I wrote ruefully right afterwards.

Mastectomy

Mammogram, mammals, milk-giving
sweet, round appendage
submitting so passively to being tested,
tried, labeled, then
brutally pierced and finally
sent to garbage-hell.

Far from the body of
that woman,
once
girl, then lover,
then wife,
then mother.

Ignored dear breast
for 15 years
after your last service
as nurturer of my son,
yet humbly serving the symmetry
of my form
as
I darted hither and yon.

Now I stare at the
ridged wound
where once you dwelt

> awed, uncertain,
> trying to see it
> as a detached symbol,
> not a disfigurement
> of
> *me.*

Instead, God sent Sister Humor once more to my rescue. Images of weird but fascinating animals from mythology, like those in Walt Disney's *Fantasia*, came to my mind. More significantly, now, every time I look up at the wounded side of Christ during Liturgy, I sense my new identification with him.

Judy's Story

Cancer was a dreaded word in our family after the early death of my mother from breast cancer and then her brother from cancer of the liver. Obviously, I was a candidate for the deadly disease, but I tried not to think about it. I did all the right things: prepared healthy foods, ate lots of organic, green vegetables, breast-fed my babies and prayed to break any family curse that might bring cancer into my body. But at the age of thirty-seven, I discovered a lump growing in my left breast.

My first response was denial. I didn't mention it to my husband, David, for months and when I finally did, I discounted his concern. Finally he insisted that I see a faith-filled Catholic doctor we knew.

The results of the mammogram were encouraging: It looked like a simple mass of tissue. Since we had no insurance, the doctor agreed that I could have the lump cut out as an outpatient under local anesthetic. However, my buoyant faith was deflated when I heard the doctor's tone of voice change as he removed the lump. I knew at that moment — before the lab even confirmed it — the mass was malignant.

As David and I walked back to the car in the hospital parking lot, we felt like the whole world had grown dark. In our minds, cancer could only mean death. We sat silently in the car, waiting for some ray of hope to pierce the blackness. Slowly and softly, David began to sing, "Rejoice in the Lord, always/ Again, I say, Rejoice." It was a deliberate act of will and obedience that made me join in the chorus. That acknowledgment of God's sovereignty in my life opened up the gates of heaven; we were soon experiencing the light of God's grace and mercy shattering the darkness. We felt assured that whatever happened, God was in charge.

This assurance went with me into the operating room on the morning of the mastectomy. My doctor, his nurse, and David prayed over me before I was wheeled through the operating room doors. The peace I experienced was more than the anesthesia could provide; it must have come through my submission and the prayers of loving brothers and sisters in Christ.

The doctor had good news for us after the surgery: it had been a localized cancer with no evidence of spreading. I would need neither chemotherapy nor radiation. As David and I walked hand-in-hand back to the parking lot after the doctor's report, we realized that we had gone through the fire — and survived.

We sat in the car and David started singing, loudly this time, "Rejoice in the Lord, always/Again, I say, Rejoice." I joined in joyfully and then we offered a prayer of thanksgiving and praise to the God who promised that he would always be with us.

In the following weeks, in spite of my dreadful jokes about my asymmetrical torso, I found that the Lord was teaching us about his presence in our lives. As a Christian, I realized, I have nothing to fear from "the valley of the shadow of death" because that was what it was: merely a shadow. Jesus overcame death on the cross and I have eternal life awaiting me.

Since that surgery, I have had another child (whom I breast-fed), discovered a heart problem and had two lumpectomies (one benign, one malignant). There were many dark moments and times when the Eucharist and the prayers of my husband and others were my only spiritual strength. The sacrament of the Anointing of the Sick also brightened a shadowy period. Yet every time I reached out to Christ, I knew he was there for me, bearing my pain with me, facing the gates of death for me.

I can't say that I'm not afraid of dying, but death no longer has an icy grip on my heart. Cancer is no longer an unmentionable word. My submission to God's will, no matter how unpleasant it seemed, became the way to attain the strength and grace I needed at each moment.

Christ comes to each of us at our worst times . . . in the way he chooses. Sometimes he comes not with any comforting imagery, but with a deeper understanding of the faith he had in his Father when he cried out from his cross, "My God, my God, why have you abandoned me?"

By looking not in the looking glass but in the mirror of Christ, we find the love that passes all understanding and the grace to endure until the glorious finale of our eternal reward, when God will "wipe away every tear."

Judy is a wife, mother, farmer, writer, and calligrapher devoted to living a simple Franciscan lifestyle in Ohio.

Chapter Six

Sue Norris

"I"—Not "We": Widowhood

Ronda: When I came to teach at Franciscan University of Steubenville as a new widow, everyone said "you must meet Sue Norris, she's a widow, too and a fascinating, sensitive, spiritual woman. What was said was all true, and she became my friend and mentor. What she told me of her own way to hold hands with God in the darkness of being a widow had so much light that I begged her to write it all out for you to benefit from as well.

"Why is that bird still singing?" My life had halted three hours earlier when my husband died suddenly. How was it possible that the rest of the world continued? This was the first thing that hit me, and hit me hard: The march of time is absolutely inexorable. I became aware of two worlds, mine and that other one out there that I used to be connected with. Well, I thought I was connected; at least it seemed familiar, but it now appeared hardly to touch me. A fog and thousands of miles separated us.

"My life is buried there too," I thought, as I stood by my husband's grave some days later, after his funeral. And in a certain sense that was absolutely true; the life I had known during my marriage and up to that point had certainly gone forever. I was no longer somebody's wife, half of a partnership, always with another to consider, with that other in turn loving, supporting, and encouraging me, being there for me, and with the vocation of becoming one with this other. I was now a single — again — and yet with so many additional responsibilities and pains.

The pains were not only from my loss but from all the unfinished business that it seemed would now *not* be finished. What could I do about all those things I wish I hadn't said, or that he had said and I hadn't understood? I was aware of the pain of these questions; I was aware also that the time to examine them was escaping me. Time itself refused to stop and allow me that space I felt I needed to catch my breath. How could we ever come to grips with all this pain? But no, here was my first lesson: "We" were not going to come to grips — "I" was.

So there were the first two adjustments: Living with the tension between a life that had gone and the appearance of existence that remained, and then the fact that it was I alone who would find my way through this maze. At this point I must pay the warmest tribute to my friends who instinctively knew that all they had to do was be there and hold me. They didn't have to find answers or come up with "solutions"; they simply had to be there even if I was at times withdrawn and numb, to let me cry or question. And be there they were, even though I can see now how great the cost was to them. It is almost as hard to watch those you love suffer and simply accompany them — silently loving though you have no "pat" answers — as it is to go through the pain yourself.

I came to real anger with God. Being a Christian is about becoming integrated, whole, and now through no fault of my own, being bereaved was to become at once split, disjointed, shattered, scattered. It was apparently to lose at one blow all the wholeness and integration achieved so far. So I hadn't "just" lost my husband, I'd lost myself as well. It just wasn't fair. All the tools I'd painfully acquired through the years to deal with such pain as the disintegration I was currently experiencing within myself had simply flown out of the window. To be bereaved is to die without dying; it is to lose everything you have known up to that point, but to continue as though it were not in fact all passed; it is to find that life has stopped but you have to continue walking, seemingly legless; it is to love your children and friends still, and yet to have no heart, no feeling; it is to hear sounds and yet have no understanding of their meaning; it is to find one's memory, long- and short-term, has gone on holiday.

This was my experience in the first weeks and months of being a widow, and I imagine at least some of that will ring true for all who must walk through this particular valley. As the weeks went by it got worse; there were these two compartments, pain with sorrow and "normal," only normal wasn't normal. Normal now was as a single, truncated-feeling person, half of whom had disappeared. And I was aware of deep fear. What happens when the two compartments come together? Integration and wholeness or unbearable pain?

"Pick up the pieces left over so that nothing gets wasted." What was that quiet whisper in the recesses of my heart? What part of my past did that little reminder come from? Yes, I remembered. Years earlier, God planted that phrase, (Jn 6:12), in my heart in the middle of a painful personal crisis, and here it was again. For a second time it would be my anchor, but now through a much greater storm. I would learn at a deeper level how God's word truly is "alive and active" in this world of the twentieth century. More to the point, his word is "alive and active" in my own life. What I found remarkable is that for a second time it came to be the introduction to a new chapter. The pieces that were left were reworked, and there came indeed to be "twelve baskets left over."

This seems to be something we learn individually only through the concrete circumstances of our lives — if we are willing. God's word can be for you, personally, an absolutely unshakable rock, and at the same time a source of tremendous life, vitality, and excitement. Of course this comes about gradually, and often painfully, as this situation demonstrates, but happen it does. At the time I remembered "Pick up the pieces," I was not able to meditate but simply called those words to mind from time to time. And that was enough. God did his gentle healing work silently, gradually.

As I looked at my life, all it seemed to consist of was a collection of fragments, not a coherent whole. There certainly wasn't any sort of flow about it. I must tell you straight off that there was no magic, immediate resolution or coming together of anything that resembled a pattern. In my journal three months into my life as a widow I was obviously quite lost, saying "I'm not myself, but who then am I?" It was like being an observer of my own life — detached, uninvolved, almost unfeeling, numb. I was the same being, inside the same skin, yet this self was different, more fluid, vulnerable and therefore more open to being molded. I knew a great need for protection, but I knew who was doing the molding — God!

I trusted so, and somehow I knew that I just had to live day by day — not to push myself into anything but to live gently — quite a change from the energetic person I had been! But it was right, and somehow a new peace entered me, along with the sorrow. God also gave loving personal signs of his presence, that he was in control, even in this valley. I think the most powerful sign was in a dream. I was six months into this period of widowhood when the word "courage" appeared spelled out in red capital letters across a clouded sky — and then next day came news that one of my dearest and most supportive friends had died suddenly. A further blow, yet that dream reminded me that God was holding my hand through it all.

If you are reading this as a widow, he is walking with you, too. Sometimes we don't recognize the signs of his presence as they can be so gentle, like the still small voice Elijah heard (I Kgs 19:12). At other times we close ourselves off from him through anger that he would allow this sorrow along this journey. But this does not stop his coming. We are all such controllers, for all we may say our life is God's and mean it. When it comes to the crunch, we really don't like him interfering in these uninvited and dreadful ways. We totally forget that life is an ongoing journey; we have not arrived. It is a melting pot: Have we not for years sung, "Melt me, mold me?" Well, here it is, the melting; and yes, it's fiery.

But he is the Potter, we are the clay, and here is another image from God's word that becomes concrete for us. The most appropriate example is in Jeremiah 18:4 which reads: "And whenever the vessel he [the potter] was making came out wrong, as happens with the clay handled by potters, he would start afresh and work it into another vessel, as potters do." The Lord goes on to say: "Can I not do to you what this potter has done? Yes, as the clay is in the potter's hand, so you are in mine."

The Potter breaks and remakes, even a seemingly complete shattering like this. Let us look for a moment at that passage, as there are several wonderful truths in it which are as real for our lives as they were in the analogy God is making to Jeremiah. (The word becoming "alive and active" again.) God uses the same clay — nothing gets wasted. Hear that again: *Nothing gets wasted.* I had no idea whatsoever how the disintegration I was going through could be anything other than useless, and I did not recognize the new shape, this new being that was emerging. She was being made from the very same lump of clay — something deep down was continuous. But I am not the Potter, the creator. I am the one being molded and fashioned into "the image and likeness" of Jesus, who is to be the eldest of many brothers and sisters (Rom 8:29).

What is "wrong" with the pot that I am is that I am damaged, by all the vicissitudes of my life as well as my own sinfulness, and that I am not yet that perfect being whom Jesus sees, knows, and loves. But he is forming me into that person. My "wrongness" is my share in the effects of original sin, and not the presence of something depraved at the core, since we know that everything that God makes is good.

I am in the hands of the Potter; the Potter who stretched out his arms on the cross for me, whose hands were pierced by nails for me. Yes, this Potter understands and actually shares my suffering; he is not merely an objective observer. Isn't this precisely what it means in Isaiah 49:16: "See, I have branded you on the palms of my hands"? And what is absolutely crucial is that this Potter, my crucified Potter, knows resurrection. Is this not resurrection, to receive at his hands a new life? As a wise person once said to me, "There can be no resurrection without a death." And the bereaved find their first experience of resurrection while still on this earth. Just as in this life our losses — small and large — prepare us for the final loss, our own death, so surely new beginnings are like mini-resurrections.

However, the resurrection following widowhood does not arrive within three days — three years may be a more realistic estimation. A struggle is involved. But the cracks in the pot that I am, especially the brokenness I was experiencing as a widow, do heal as he remolds.

Another passage to meditate on is Ephesians 2:10, which describes us as "God's work of art." Unfortunately we get painted over with a lot of different colors, and we also add our own hues and shadows. God has to remove "our" picture to reveal His own unique work of art — his original who is alive with color and form — vibrant, individual, vital. C.S. Lewis wrote "What we call the end is often the beginning." The end of one era also carries with it the seeds of a new one. The cleaning of a painting reveals something quite new and alive underneath the accumulation of dust or additions over the years.

Apart for "being with" those passages of Scripture that really ministered to my aching soul, I wish I had asked for the Sacrament of the Sick. We bereaved are wounded and hurting and need to meet the Lord in this healing sacrament — we need to be ministered to by his body, the Church, and to receive strength from the Lord. I didn't receive this sacrament until some years later, when I asked for it as part of a process of healing of memories, and the healing was so beautiful that I wished I had thought to ask earlier. I would like to see this healing opportunity routinely offered to all bereaved people.

After the death of my husband, I lost my singing voice. Quite unexpectedly, my voice was renewed and I could sing again. (This ability had apparently gone on holiday with my faculty of memory. I regret to say that my memory is still somewhere "out there"!) It was so touching to realize that the Lord was interested in all the tiny details of my life, even those I hadn't bothered about, and in blessing me in surprising ways. In my grief, it simply never occurred to me to ask him to let me sing again; in his love, he gave me what I needed.

Sue Norris is a widow and mother with an M.A. in theology from Franciscan University of Steubenville. She is presently a writer and pastoral associate in England, the land of her birth.

Chapter Seven

Dorothy Miranda Neamand

Worse Than Death: Divorce

*Ronda: I met Dorothy at Franciscan University of Steubenville where she was working as an academic staff person. As she typed survival stories for this book, I got to know her better. Pretty soon I was asking her if she would write her own story for **Holding Hands With God**. She agreed. I think you will find it as hopeful as I did.*

Rick and I were married, in a civil ceremony, June 1, 1962. We met through mutual friends while we were both serving in the Army. Rick was on orders to go to Thailand for a year, and we wanted to get married before he left.

When Rick and I first entered the covenant of marriage, I considered it was for life. The words "until death do us part" have a deep meaning for me. Rick had no church affiliation, while I had been raised Roman Catholic. My parents didn't go to church, and neither did any of my relatives. I usually went with the neighbors and their children. When we moved to a new neighborhood in my teens, I dropped out completely.

My concept of God was still childlike in some ways. I knew he made me because he loved me, but I had great trouble believing this. My childhood was one of a chaotic home life and constant warnings that if I was bad, I would go to hell and God only showed mercy to his saints, one of which I would never be. My parents and brothers constantly reminded me of how unattractive I was and no one would ever want me, let alone God. My self-esteem was as low as a slug on the sidewalk. I never did anything right to please anyone.

When I was a teen, I was so hungry for love I would go out with anyone who asked me. It was hard for me to believe anyone saw more in me than what was visible. This concept of myself continued for a lifetime. I was grateful to Rick for wanting me enough to marry me.

My fantasy of marriage was to have the perfect husband, children, house, and so on. My role models were the television shows of the 1950s, where all the problems were solved in a half an hour, and the mothers portrayed in the programs were almost saints. What a shock when I found out I had married a career military man and we would not live in the same house for the next hundred years, he would not always come home at five o'clock, our children would not be perfect, we would move every two years or so, and we would leave a host of friends all over the world.

As both of us were of an independent nature, the adjustment to marriage was difficult. Rick was gone the first year and that didn't make it any easier. My mother died of cancer a few weeks after he left, so I stayed home and took care of my younger sister and brother, as my father's career as a merchant seaman kept him away for weeks. I learned to be strong early in life and so moved right into my mother's role of housekeeper and babysitter. When Rick returned, we were stationed at Fort Hood, Texas. Our whole marriage seemed to be one long struggle. Rick was the youngest of eight children and had no role model for what a husband is responsible for except for bringing home the paycheck. The rest of the duties belonged to the wife. I did not want to be strong any more. I wanted to be the kind of wife who just took care of the children and the house, not financial burdens too. But I was given no choice in the matter.

We had been married two years when our daughter Kimberly was conceived. I knew I wanted to have her baptized, so I started going back to church before she arrived. I had a great fear of dying in childbirth. I don't know why, but I knew I wanted my child dedicated to God. First I had to get myself back on track, so I became a regular churchgoer again. Rick consented to marry me in the Church, which we did on July 16, 1964, a month before Kimberly was born. Our second child, Michelle, was born in Frankfort, Germany, in 1969.

In our tenth year of marriage, 1972, we were stationed on Okinawa, and we both were encouraged to attend a Cursillo, which we did in 1974. Rick had joined the Church the year before. Our priest encouraged us to attend a Marriage Encounter at Fort Hood when we returned to the states two years later. However, instead of helping, after that we seemed to focus more on our problems and differences.

We belonged to various prayer groups through the years which helped us stay focused on the Lord most of the time. However, when we moved to upstate New York in 1983, there was no prayer group for us to join. Rick worked a lot of weekends training military reserves all over the state, and the girls and I attended church without him.

By the twenty-eighth year, our life was utter chaos. Our daughters were in college, and I had lived my life for them, as a volunteer girl scout leader, CCD teacher, room mother, library volunteer, and more. Rick said I said yes to everyone but him. We were trying very hard to have a relationship but I had been in control too long and was not able to step back. It was quite obvious neither one of us was going to change. Our marriage lasted twenty-nine years, the last nine years almost a constant battle of me trying to pass responsibility to Rick but never really trusting him to take any.

Rick retired from the Army in 1988 with thirty years service. He was totally unhappy and full of anger, which erupted onto me. While we tried a six-month separation to see what we really wanted, Rick met someone else and wanted a divorce, even though we were both practicing Catholics, so to speak. I cried to my priest, and he suggested I go ahead and give Rick his divorce and apply for an annulment. I entered a therapy group, and by this time had taken a course as a home health aide. I did not have enough self-esteem to think I could do much of anything, but I went to work and tried to make it on my own.

The dictionary defines the word "divorce" as 1) the legal termination of a marriage; and 2) the separation of things that were together. But, the dictionary doesn't describe what a person may feel following this "separation of things that were together."

Divorce is an acceptable practice in today's society. No longer a rare occurrence, it doesn't carry the stigma of a failed marriage. We all know someone who is divorced for one reason or another. Some couples enter marriage with the idea that if it doesn't work, divorce is always an option. In fact, for Christians, divorce shouldn't even be considered an option to working on the marriage union. A working relationship is a full-time commitment.

Divorce was total devastation for me. I had to find a whole new identity for myself, plus find out what I really believed in. I realized the man I had married was no more, and only this man full of anger was left. Rick blamed me for the things he never got to do or be. Of course, as a co-dependent, I took the blame.

Divorce is worse than death. The other half of the marriage union is still alive, and I feared meeting him, and another woman, each time I went out the front door. Each time the phone rang, I held my breath until I was sure it wasn't Rick. Yet, a part of me saddened with this realization. The dream was dead, the dream that we would grow old together. Suddenly I was alone. Marriage makes two people one, and the part of me that had been cruelly severed was raw and bleeding profusely. I kept thinking, "If this man who knows me better than anyone else in the world doesn't love me, how can anyone else?"

I thought myself unlovable, worthless, not fit to be alive. I considered suicide, but my mind filled with objections: My daughters would find my dead body in the house; too many people seemed to be counting on me and the commitments I had made; I couldn't think of a way to do it painlessly; and I feared eternal hell fire. Because I can't swim, I did think of walking into the lake I lived near, but again my mind rejected the idea. I guess my will to live was stronger than my will to die. I kept hearing the phrase my daughter learned in high school: "Suicide is a permanent solution to a temporary problem." With the pain so intense in the beginning, working out livable solutions was tough.

After I knew our marriage was really over, I had trouble even thinking, let alone feeling glad to be alive. Tears were my constant companion. It was hard to imagine anything could get me past the pain. The raw agony of being severed in two is hard enough to deal with. The first day I walked in a park near my home and sat on a bench. The birds were singing, the sky was blue, there was a soft, spring breeze. It amazed me that God's world was still going on. It should have been gray and dreary with his tears mingling with mine. Why wasn't the whole world crying with me?

Sometimes friends hurt me more than helped. They don't know what to say or are superficial, if they have not experienced divorce themselves. The worst phrase is "Have a nice day." I wanted to tell the speaker what to do with that remark, and it wasn't nice. I felt "nice days" were over for me.

I realized I had two options at this point of my life. The first one was to crawl in bed, cover up my head, and stay there until a) I starved to death; b) the pain went away; or c) God gave me a reason to get up again. The second option was to stay on my feet, learn to live with the pain, and go on with my life. I chose the second option, although there were days I seriously considered the first.

Rick left in mid-April, 1990, and I didn't hear from his lawyer until September. The pain had dulled a bit because I was in school and had my studies to occupy me, most of the time. (I had waited all my life for another dream that was becoming a reality. I wanted to go to college to see if I was as intelligent as I thought.

God made it possible for me to pursue this dream. I started at the local junior college in January, 1990.)

The day I received the lawyer's letter telling me Rick was pursuing the divorce, I was once again plunged into the depths of despair. The wound that had scabbed over was opened once again. That night I was supposed to meet friends at a county fair, driving the thirty miles to meet them. I picked up the phone and called to tell them I wasn't coming, so my friend John (who belonged to the same therapy group as I did) came over and picked me up. He just let me talk and stayed with me the entire evening, by my side, supporting me and listening to my heart break anew.

When Rick left, I knew why God had me join a therapy group. The group supported me through the first weeks and months, and without these eleven people reaffirming me as a person, I have no idea how much harder it would have been. I thank God for them, for while I trusted the Lord to see me through, I seemed to need a living, breathing person to hug me sometimes. The two members I knew best were Chris and John. I lived with Chris' mother as she and I were friends before the divorce. She was a Catholic and going through the same thing I was — her husband left her. (Sometimes we joked about having to hang a black flag on the house when we both had spells of depression.)

Chris and I saw each other outside of the group nights, and he, too, was going through a divorce. I felt like the plague of divorce had hit almost everyone I came in contact with. John was a man in his forties and had never been married. He was lonely and came to see Chris and me a lot. When John asked me to go to a fair with him, I was shocked! I couldn't believe he wanted to be seen with me. I knew Rick didn't want me anymore; why in the world would anyone else? I was self-conscious with John at the fair and couldn't relax enough to enjoy myself. I hadn't been out with anyone but Rick in more than thirty years.

For about three weeks I imagined myself in love with John, with all the silly emotions of youth. God did show me it wasn't love but simply a reaction to someone being nice to me in my time of vulnerability. So few people had been nice to me. I think that is why I was so surprised when John first asked me out. We became platonic friends, since I was too steeped in my beliefs to do otherwise.

I was ripe for the New Age Movement. In October, 1990, a few of my therapy group had attended a seminar called "Life stream." The brochure was sort of vague. I knew I was hungry for something that I didn't seem to be getting from the Lord. I had no support from a prayer group or any other organization in the Church. In my vulnerable stage, I was willing to try anything to help me through the pain.

"Life stream" is a weekend seminar. The thrust is to feel good about yourself. The family who runs the seminar has done extensive studies in human nature. We all had low self-esteem. The weekends are teasers designed to get people to spring for the weeklong seminar that is quite expensive. I do hope the Lord will forgive me for comparing these weekends to religious retreats that I have been on. The emotions are involved in so many ways, which is where most people are caught by any movement. I went to the weeklong seminar the second week in July, 1991. The week was quite intense. We exercised daily and were allowed only four hours sleep per night. We had to give up cigarettes, aspirin, anything not a prescription drug, red meat, alcohol, and caffeine. I think the method used makes people quite vulnerable. I know I was.

The thrust of the seminars was to teach a method of meditation called "centering." We sat with our eyes closed and imagined ourselves in our favorite scene. I really think what saved me was when I centered, within myself, I always took Jesus Christ with me. I never went alone. I think what we were supposed to get from this exercise was positive thinking about ourselves to boost our self-esteem. My self-esteem was helped, and I lost a bit of my shyness around people. But I was at the University of Steubenville only a week, arriving in Fall 1991, when I repented of this New Age Movement and asked for God's forgiveness, which he granted me in his mercy and love for me.

My divorce became final in August, 1991. The week my divorce came through, my wounds were once again open and bleeding. I slowly became aware of a sadness settling in my heart. During counseling in my sophomore year, I was told it would always be there. It took me six months to say the "D" word. The worst part was being alone once I left the campus. I would leave school on Friday afternoon at four and not go back until ten Monday morning. I went to Mass on campus, but it was hard sitting alone every week. I finally talked to one of the priests when I had missed Mass one Sunday because I felt so alone, even there. He told me I would never "fit in" with the students because of the age difference, but he also asked me to think about why I went to Mass in the first place. I should remember I was there to worship the Lord, and after that talk, when I went to Mass I concentrated on worshiping the Lord whether I was alone or not. It has made a world of difference. No Mass is boring or mundane, for I am spending time with my favorite person, God, and am there only to give him glory and praise.

I stopped sending Christmas cards to our mutual friends, because I felt so ashamed of our failed marriage. I even threw out my address book and started a new one.

The day I cleaned out my mementos of our marriage was really sad. As I read and reread each card or letter from Rick or picked up a souvenir from one of our trips, the tears flowed anew. The pain was almost unbearable. I was drained emotionally by the time I was done. I had to spend the rest of the day in my room, alone, working through the pain of my emotions. Just about the time I felt my pain was healing, Rick sent me a Christmas card in 1991. My emotions took over again. He hadn't sent a Christmas card to anyone ever before. I wrote him a letter and asked why, but he didn't answer. As time went on, the pain grew less but didn't completely disappear.

With a divorce, people go through the same stages as with death. Anger is one. On the days when I had to get my allergy shots at the nearby army base, I would often be so angry about the way Rick dumped me, like a bag of garbage, that I swore if I met Rick on the road I would run both of us off and hopefully kill us. Of course I thought he was happy with his new love, and there were places I couldn't go for fear I would see them together. On my angry days, I would say to myself, I'll spit on them. On my depressed days, I thought I would probably fall at his feet and beg him to take me back. To keep myself from either shame, I just avoided the places I thought I might run into Rick.

The problem of dealing with the different stages of denial, anger, depression, bargaining, and acceptance is that there is no set pattern of progress. When one stage is worked through and another is moved into, sometimes, a yo-yo effect takes place. I just know I took three steps forward at times and then regressed two steps. Fortunately, once a stage is worked through and gone back to, the time spent in that stage is shortened the next time. This process can take years.

The sadness never leaves; it just lessens in intensity with time. It becomes a part of you, as if it has always been inside. I have been told it will always be a part of me. I guess how I learn to live with this sadness is up to me. I can let it cripple me or help me in my walk with my God as he uses me in ministering to others in pain. I do have more compassion now. My pain makes me want to reach out and help someone else work through the pain. I have learned to be a better listener because I now know sometimes that's all that's needed. The person in pain usually is the one who needs to talk. Talking out the pain can sometimes help put life into perspective.

As I progressed through school, my self-esteem grew and so did my self-confidence. I discovered talents I was not aware of. I learned to love myself and let others love me. I've learned to ask for help when I need it, which has not always been easy for me. My understanding of God grew up and took root in my life. My relationship with him is now in order. I want only his will for my life. I have quit whining when life isn't exactly the way I want it, for I know God's plan for me is going to be much better than I can even imagine. I have learned what waiting on the Lord really is. It is well worth it.

The university afforded me several opportunities. I finally got my chance to act on the stage — well chapel anyway — by being in *The Living Stations* two years in a row. My friends said they really thought I was crying when Jesus said to me, on the way to the cross, "Weep not for me, Mother, but instead weep for your children." I helped with orientation for new students three semesters and was blessed. During my senior year, I sponsored an RCIA candidate. I often wonder why I waited so long to do it.

I discovered that Christianity is a way of life, not an attempt to be holy. More than words, my life should be a testimony for Christ. I don't expect to be perfect until after I go home to live with the Lord and he "finishes" me. Now, I just try to rejoice through the sanding and polishing.

I did not pursue an annulment after all. There was always a reason to put it off. For instance, I did have the money but could I really afford it? There was going to be more pain . . . did I really want to make the marriage break final? I couldn't come to a decision one way or the other, so I just kept procrastinating.

I had not talked to Rick for four years when he called one night for Kimberly (she had joined me at the university to work on her master's degree in counseling). I answered the phone and felt butterflies float through my stomach when I finally heard the voice I longed to hear. We chatted about my classes and our mutual interests for about an hour. Rick sent me a couple of books and called to see if they arrived. Whenever he called for Kimberly, we both usually talked to Rick. I was starting to wonder what was going on, and while I *knew* God was in charge, I sure would have liked a hint. During one phone call, I mentioned spring break, and Rick invited us to visit him in Waterdown, New York. He had already asked to come to graduation in May, but Kimberly and I had told him no. I wasn't sure how I would react, and it *was* my big day, too. I had worked four long years and wanted nothing to spoil it for me.

Kimberly and I decided to go to New York. I wasn't sure

how I would feel seeing Rick again. God had not taken away my feelings for Rick no matter how much I begged him. I had come to realize each person deserves to be loved for themselves, not for what they do or for who we want them to be. I had never loved Rick that way and I was saddened by the fact. Now, I felt ready to, if it was possible.

The visit was painful for me. I kept wondering why Rick had invited us. He told me, midweek, he liked living alone, which told me he didn't invite us because he still had feelings for me. I went off by myself and finally came to the point of acceptance of the fact we were apart for life. It was freeing in a way because then I could let go of the hope we would eventually get back together. From that time on, I started to plan my life with only me in the picture.

When I finally "let go" of Rick, God was able to move, and he did. When Rick came for graduation, he saw me in my own element, with my friends, and he saw how much I had grown in the four years we had been apart. I was more secure in my own identity and more self-confident; I no longer need to be in control of every situation in life. We talked more in that weekend than we had, it seemed, in our marriage. Rick had grown also, in self-awareness. He and I both forgave each other for our own part in the divorce and the pain. The visit turned out to be a healing process for us. God was in control and we were both willing to let him be. By the time Rick left, we were seeing the good in each other, and the anger was gone.

In July, 1994, I was off for three weeks and took a trip to New York for one of them. Rick and I were alone and able to discuss whatever we desired. We really got into some pain. We kept in touch after that by phone once or twice a week. We rediscovered all the interests we had in common. We had both mellowed and the things that seemed so important before no longer seemed to matter. Best of all, Rick and I were able to talk without getting defensive with each other. We now knew marriage was a partnership and we both needed to work at it and be open to each other.

I joined Rick for Thanksgiving, and the girls joined us, Kimberly from New Hampshire and Michelle from New Jersey, for Christmas. It was the first time we had all been together in six years. It was so wonderful to go to Christmas Mass together.

Rick asked me to marry him on Christmas Eve, in front of the girls. We renewed our marriage vows on May twenty-seventh at the Franciscan University of Steubenville. Since neither one of us had sought an annulment, we were considered married in the Church. We went a few days before and had a civil ceremony, with only our two girls present. The renewal of vows was the real celebration for us, with all my friends present. I bought a special dress and we celebrated the Mass as though it were the first time. Afterwards, we had a small reception and departed the next day for New York, where we now live.

God is first in our lives and we thank him daily for the miracle of our marriage. We know we had adjusting to do, but we are loving each other daily, doing little things together, praying for guidance and mercy. We will be eternally grateful to God and God alone that he has given us a brand new relationship, and we will make a new dream together.

Thank you, God, for loving me
the me that was meant to be.
You brought me out of darkness and pain
And showed me how to live again.
You let me through the darkest night
when I yearned only to take flight.
You taught me how to sing and play
to rejoice in each new day.
You are my sole reason to live
when I know I have only me to give.
When the world is dark and gray
you help me face each new day.
You are my strength in times of fear
For I know you are always near.

Holding Hands With God

You know me best of all
when I stand and when I fall.
You lift me up when I am down
and make a smile out of a frown.
You give me hope when I feel none
You've taught me to walk in the Son.
You are never far away from me at all
and always answer when I call.
Best of all you let me be me
the me that was meant to be.
Amen.

Dorothy is a homemaker, volunteer, and Religious Education Coordinator for her parish. She also works with Friends of Jesus, a group in her church which helps adults who are mentally or physically challenged.

Chapter Eight

Katherine O'Brien-Johnston, Obl. OSB

A Hidden Loss: Miscarriage

Ronda: "There's a woman with small children who wants to be a writer, Ronda. She'd love to meet you." When Katherine came to visit, I was just finishing selecting sharings for "Holding Hands." I pounced on her to write this one.

When I found out I was pregnant for the second time in less than a year and a half, I was surprised and then elated. Surprised because my son, Seán, then six-and-a-half months old, was still nursing regularly. I didn't think I had much chance of becoming pregnant.

I also didn't expect it, at least not so soon, in the strange town my husband and I had moved to only three months before. We had taken ourselves and our infant son two thousand miles away from our friends and families in order to start a new life. We hadn't even unpacked everything yet, and here I was pregnant again.

Surprise soon gave way to elation as I first accepted and then joyfully embraced this blessing from God. A child, a second child, had been given me, a child that I hoped to see and hold in just a few more months. My excitement began to grow almost immediately, an excitement which my husband shared with me as we began to discuss our plans and to broadcast the news to the world. And broadcast we did, at least to our long-distant friends and families — practically everything except shouting from our rooftop.

And we began to prepare for our new child — our daughter, as we hoped and believed she would be. We picked out names, and even started talking to Seán about his new and important role as a big brother. And since we had never had an infant car seat of our own, I went out and bought one in anticipation of our future need. I beamed as Seán and I walked through the store with it, and once home, kept it where I could see it.

I was only a few weeks pregnant when Thanksgiving arrived. We had no one to celebrate with but that did not diminish our joy, for we knew that we had much to be thankful for. We planned a full meal, with turkey and all the fixings, and our preparations were underway Thanksgiving morning when the first sign of trouble appeared.

At first I felt like I had a stomachache, but then I began to feel like I was in labor. It felt like one, long contraction, and it just kept going on, and getting worse. Finally, after more than an hour, my husband decided to take me to a hospital. When we got to the hospital, the pain was so bad I could barely walk — if my husband hadn't been there to hold me up, I would have crawled across the parking lot to the front door. When I got inside, I found out that there wasn't much the doctors could do, because not only was I pregnant, I was also nursing. They did give me some medicine that allowed me to sleep a few hours, and when I awoke they were able to examine and then tell me what had happened, as much as they were able to figure it out.

Their best guess was that I had an ovarian cyst which had ruptured. I was very concerned about my baby, but they couldn't tell me anything, this early in the pregnancy. My husband, however, felt sure that we had lost the child. He said he didn't know how he knew, but he knew the child had died. I didn't know what to think, but I feared the worst, even while I was hoping for the best.

A Hidden Loss

The next two days we knew nothing more, and I had even started to think that I might still be pregnant after all, and that everything was going to turn out okay. Saturday was my birthday, which we tried to celebrate by making the turkey dinner my husband had shoved in the fridge before taking me to the hospital on Thursday. But the celebration turned sour when in the midst of it I discovered that I had miscarried.

At least, this is what I thought happened, though I was not absolutely sure for quite a while. I proceeded to have test after test, but most of them were inconclusive. I so wanted not to lose this baby, but more and more I began to believe that I had. One of the nurses marked my card "postpartum," which really hurt. I was not going to believe the worst until we knew it was true. Finally, two weeks later, in mid-December, the suspense ended. I was no longer pregnant; we had lost our second child.

In one sense, life was immediately easier. I was able to get off the emotional roller coaster I had been on. For a fortnight I had been telephoning and talking with family and with friends so often that I think some of them began to dread hearing the sound of my voice. I can't say I would have blamed them — it was a very strained time for me as I alternated between hope and despair. I tried to work and live normally and take care of Seán, but I was utterly unproductive and drifted about like a ship without a rudder. I needed to know what was going on inside me, and when I got the news, even though it was bad news, it was almost a relief. At last now I knew.

It still hurt, of course — how is a mother ever consoled for the loss of her child? — but I at least knew that my daughter was safe with God, and that nothing in this world could ever hurt her again. We named her Christina Grace. It just didn't feel right not to give her a name, although she would never need it in this world, even for a tombstone. We would never see her, never hold her, never help her to grow in love and holiness, but at least we could give her a name.

I have some friends who have done the same with their miscarried babies, but miscarriage is difficult for most people.

75

Miscarriage is a hidden loss — there is no body, no funeral, and many people think the baby isn't "real" until born. They act and speak as though there had never been a baby. And so it was with many with whom we shared our loss. Many of our friends were scandalized that we had we named her, and even more scandalized when we arranged for a Mass to be celebrated in her honor. But this, too, was something we had to do. We needed to heal, and we needed this Mass, almost as a rite of passage, for ourselves if not for Christina. It helped us to accept that our child was in heaven, that our love for her and delight in her existence had been received, and that God, in his infinite mercy and love, had received this precious child of ours in his arms and was now holding her to his bosom.

In the days and weeks following, I began to discover how common this experience is among women I know. It seems that most of the mothers I spoke with had also suffered this loss, often many times. I have long known of this in my own family — my mother had four miscarriages after giving birth to me and my sister, for example — but the reality of it, the pain, the grief, and the loss were something I never really understood until it happened to me. No one had ever talked about it. Consequently, it seemed like it had never happened — the grief and pain, I mean. The silence just impelled me to share my experience even more frequently and openly. It is somehow healing to share with someone else who has been through what you have.

One of the miscarriage stories I heard involved a woman named Louise who had made a baptismal gown and baby blanket for a relative's baby. The baby was lost late in the pregnancy and rather than pass the garments on to another child, Louise burned all that she had made. This was painful for me to hear; it felt like a negation of that baby's reality. But it was the best way Louise knew to handle the loss. It was, in a way like the Mass we had celebrated for Christina; it was the ending of a chapter, the closing of a book on the life of a loved one.

Since my miscarriage occurred shortly before Christmas and

the grief was so fresh, I added Christina's name to some of our Christmas cards. I even bought a small card with her name and its meaning on it, and attached it to our refrigerator. I wanted some reminders of her, and I wanted to let the world know that I really did once hold this child in my womb, if only for a few short weeks. She was real, and I was not about to forget her. I just couldn't act as though she had never existed.

It has been more than a year now since our child was taken from us. My husband and I still speak of her from time to time. We long planned to do something to celebrate the day which would have been her birthday, but when the time came my husband had to be out of town on an unexpected but very necessary two-month-long business trip. And then, as soon as he returned, we had to abruptly pull up stakes and move to yet another town. If Christina had been born it would have been a very difficult time for all of us, and I have sometimes wondered if maybe that is why God allowed this miscarriage to happen. We still miss her. We still speak of her — and we still cry. I sometimes look for her in the house when I am gathering up Seán to run off on some errand. The aching hole in our hearts longs to be filled. God has not given us another child yet. We wait, we hope, and we pray.

Is any loss ever fully healed? It seemed as though so many women I spoke with have never been able to heal the wounds of their losses. So many simply try to force themselves to forget, even while they acknowledge their own inability to forget their little ones. But they cannot forget, as I will not forget. In Isaiah 49, our Lord says that even if a mother forgets her own baby, He will not forget. That must mean that his love for us is great indeed, for what mother could ever truly forget her own child? I know that I cannot. I long to hold and behold my Christina in heaven. I long to meet this little one, given me as daughter, and tell her face-to-face that I love her.

Along the way, many people have shared their faith and stories with me. Three thoughts have particularly helped me to heal. Maybe they can help you or someone you know, too.

First, God works *all* things together for the good of those who love him (Rom 8:28). This can be tough to believe but I have found this true even as I endure the loss of separation. God is on our side. A priest friend told me that, in a sense, no family is complete unless they have one member in heaven. By no means was he wishing death into any house, but he was saying that those little ones are a sort of anchor for the rest of us still on this earth. And this is good. Those little ones are not truly lost to us; they are waiting to welcome us home to heaven. Now death brings something concretely joyful with it — the reunion with these little ones.

The second thing I was told that helped me was that our job, our vocation, as Christian parents is to raise up our children as children of the Most High God. And Christina is indeed God's child, so we have cause for rejoicing. We have one child reigning in heaven with God. Nothing can separate her from God. Our parental mission with her is complete.

And third, I was reminded that those little ones are able to pray for us. I find myself calling upon Christina's aid often, especially for her big brother and her mama who miss her so much. I can speak to her throughout the day, knowing that she will intercede for us before the throne of God. This has created a relationship between us, albeit a limited one, that can continue to grow.

Love your children — from the very first moment you discover their existence within your womb. Do as Jesus did — love recklessly, fully, with your whole being, not counting the cost. And do not be afraid; God is indeed with you. He will bless your love, no matter what befalls you.

God bless you!

Katherine is a lay member of a Benedictine Community, who is both a mother and a writer. She and her family currently reside in San Diego.

Chapter Nine

Maria Veronika Healy

Worry and Anxiety — Peace and Trust: Complications in Pregnancy, Delivery, and Infant Distress

Ronda: In the 60s, we used to say of another: "She's such a beautiful person." Maria is a dear friend, greatly admired for her nobility and spirituality of soul. I am happy to "share" her with you as she tells about a suffering many more experience than we usually think.

I especially felt Jesus holding my hand while I was walking on the path of suffering in the experience surrounding the pregnancy, birth, and first few weeks of life of my fifth child, Lenore. Eight years ago, when we found out I was pregnant, we were ecstatic. We had four wonderful and healthy children, but then three miscarriages. We never found out the reason for the miscarriages, each in the thirteenth week of pregnancy. Needless to say, we were somewhat apprehensive about this new pregnancy. Would I be able to carry this baby to term and hold it in my arms? I knew I had to put my trust in God, who sustains all things. I had to pray for trust and abandonment to God's will every day.

After three weeks of pregnancy, I began bleeding. I was put on bed rest for the next five weeks. This was quite a challenge, especially with four children ages ten, nine, six, and four and school beginning in one week for the three older children. My husband suddenly had a lot of extra work piled on his shoulders. I on the other hand had a lot of time to think and pray — and to knit a large number of little hats, pullovers, and shawls for my children's assorted teddy bears.

After the five weeks of bed rest, my pregnancy went well until the seventh month when a bad case of the flu with a nasty cough put me into the hospital for a few days. The threatening contractions calmed down and everything was well again. About a week before the due date, while I was praying for a safe delivery, I heard an inner voice asking me, "Will you accept this child even if it may not be perfect?" At first I was very worried, but then I realized that it was only by God's grace that I had been able to come this far in the pregnancy.

I asked our Lord for strength and prayed, "Your will be done." On April 7, 1989 I finally went into labor. It was long and hard, much more difficult than my previous four labors, but finally our Lenore was born. Fortunately, the doctor had moved me into the delivery room from the birthing room. "With your history of miscarriages, I'd feel safer having you in the delivery room," he said. It proved to be prophetic.

Lenore was born with her umbilical cord wrapped tightly around her little neck. They had to cut it immediately. I was so happy to finally have another girl! Lenore uttered one cry, turned purple and stopped moving her arms and legs. Everybody raced to her. "What's happening with my baby?" I asked, but everyone was so busy assessing Lenore that I got no answer. Our next-door neighbor, an anesthesiologist, just happened to be on call that day and he put Lenore on the respirator immediately to get oxygen into her little body. Then they wheeled away our newborn baby daughter. I didn't even get a good look at her.

Our pediatrician came to us with tears in her eyes and told

us, "Your child has transposition of the great vessels, which is incompatible with life. We have to get her to Children's Hospital in Pittsburgh. I have already called the helicopter. They can do miracles there. She has a chance."

We were stunned. We couldn't believe it. After three miscarriages we finally had our baby and now we might lose her. A priest from the Franciscan University of Steubenville rushed over and gave her an emergency baptism, which was a great consolation for us.

Before Lenore flew off in the helicopter, she was brought in to me so that I could say good-bye. Doctors and nurses trailed behind her with an oxygen tank. One of the doctors from the helicopter team was hand-pumping her oxygen. Lenore looked so innocent and beautiful, even if purple. I stroked her on the forehead through one of the little openings of the incubator. Then they took her away. I heard the whirling of the helicopter blades and from my recovery room bed I saw the helicopter take off.

I thought my heart would break. Will I ever be able to hold her in my arms, to hug her and cuddle with her and love her? Will we ever see her alive again? We prayed for help and strength and for healing and protection for Lenore and for us.

In Pittsburgh, they attempted a balloon heart catheterization procedure. They wanted to keep the little hole between the heart chambers which normally closes right after birth open in order to facilitate the exchange of oxygen-poor blood and oxygen-rich blood. They explained to us that in transposition of the great vessels, the arteries grow out wrong from the heart. Thus the oxygen-rich blood from the lungs goes right back to the lungs and the oxygen-poor blood goes right back to the rest of the body which is starved for oxygen. The oxygen-poor blood goes to the kidneys, brain, and other organs, causing tremendous damage.

At 3:30 a.m, less than fourteen hours after Lenore's birth, we received a call from the pediatric cardiologist telling us the balloon procedure had not been successful. His voice broke.

Success would have allowed a delay of a few weeks before doing the major surgery Lenore needed, which would have given her time to recover from her birth. But now he was asking for permission to do immediate open-heart surgery. It would involve a complete switch of the great vessels and the coronary arteries and was needed as soon as possible. The surgery might save her, though nothing could be guaranteed.

Lenore was one of only a few who could actually qualify for this operation because all her other body systems were in great shape. They scheduled the operation to begin Sunday morning, just thirty-eight hours after her birth. With heavy hearts we gave the permission. We wanted to give her a chance, even though this complete-switch operation was relatively new and Lenore would be one of the youngest patients ever.

I was still in the hospital recuperating on Saturday when Michael left to take the other four children to Pittsburgh to see their little sister. They all had prayed for this baby, and we wanted them to know that Lenore Healy really existed. Each child was able to go into intensive care one by one and see Lenore and stroke her gently on her forehead or leg and pray for her.

On Sunday morning at seven Michael took me out of the hospital in Ohio to be with Lenore for her 8:30 a.m. operation in Pittsburgh. I was weak, in pain, and emotionally exhausted, but I had to see Lenore and be with her.

Lenore was a ghastly gray-yellow color and almost lifeless. The doctors had put her on paralyzing drugs so she would not waste any energy. Her oxygenation rate was at twenty percent, which for grown-ups would be deadly. I couldn't help thinking, "What if Lenore survives this operation, but is brain damaged or develops cerebral palsy because of her low oxygenation rate?"

I called her by her name, sang to her, stroked her little legs and arms, and prayed as hard as I have ever prayed in my life. I prayed for God's protection and blessings over her. I prayed that her guardian angel would assist the surgeons and anesthesiologists and guide their hands.

Then they came to get her and my heart felt as if it was ripped to pieces. "Will I ever see you again, dear baby? Will you be alive when you come back to us?" All of a sudden a great sense of peace filled my heart. I felt sure she would survive the operation. Michael too felt very peaceful even though, considering the facts, we had no reason to feel this way at all. I know this peace came from God, and while we spent the next ten hours in a mixture of worry and anxiety, we also knew peacefulness and trust.

Just thirty-eight hours old and Lenore was having open heart surgery and was on a heart-lung machine! The doctors opened her chest and sternum and switched her pulmonary and coronary arteries using microscopic surgery. By God's providence, the best team of pediatric-thoracic cardiologists at Pittsburgh Children's Hospital just happened to be on call that day and devoted their entire Sunday to saving Lenore. I will never forget Doctor Sewers and his team. After she had been in surgery about eight hours, we got word that Lenore had passed the operation with flying colors and we would be able to see her within the hour. We were so happy and grateful and thankful to God. But then one hour passed and then two and still no Lenore. The doctor came and informed us that there were complications with her pulmonary artery. They had to open Lenore twice more to correct bleeding problems with her pulmonary artery.

When we went to her, she was in critical condition of course but she was a beautiful pink, rosy color and the doctors were quite pleased, even though they could still give no guarantees that she would pull through it all. We were quite traumatized by the more than two dozen IVs, tubes, and monitoring lines which seemed to come out of every part of her body and were all hooked up to computers. There was only one little spot on her lower left leg where I could stroke her gently. She looked so tiny, vulnerable, and innocent and yet had to endure so much! The respirator made strange noises — artificial and disconcerting. We prayed over her.

Every day for three weeks we visited Lenore in the Intensive Care unit. At first she seemed to improve a bit every day and came off some of the IVs. After about two weeks they tried to wean her off the respirator, which unfortunately was unsuccessful. That afternoon was frightening. I sang to her as I usually did. I called to her, "Lenore, Lenore." Usually she would open her little brown eyes and establish eye contact with me. This day, she was too weak. When our eyes met, she seemed to look right through me. She appeared too weak to respond. I felt as if ice-cold fingers were gripping my heart.

That night Michael and I broke down and cried and prayed, "Help us, dear Lord. Please either take Lenore to heaven to be with you or help her to get off the respirator. But your will be done." We felt like we could not go on like this any longer. Recently, we had heard of a baby who had never grown strong enough to get off the respirator and had just slowly withered away and died. All these fears ran through our minds.

When we went to visit Lenore in the hospital the following day, she was *off* the respirator! She had an oxygen tube in her nose, but otherwise she was breathing on her own! We were stunned, happy, and deeply grateful to God. The doctors had given Lenore a richer diet through her feeding IV, but they did not quite understand why *this time* she was strong enough to get off the respirator and stay off it. We knew. What a gracious answer to our prayers! What love! What mercy! We thanked God from the depths of our hearts.

My heart ached to hold Lenore in my arms. Finally Lenore got out of the Intensive Care unit and into the normal pediatric station. Finally I could hold her and kiss her and snuggle with her. She still had two IVs and an oxygen tube and could not yet eat normally. She also had to receive a large amount of blood by transfusion during her first critical two-and-one-half weeks of life. We would not know for many months whether any of that blood was tainted.

Just in hope that it would be needed, I had been pumping my breasts four times a day for the past three weeks in order to build up my milk supply. I remember racking my brain whether I actually should do this. "If Lenore dies," I thought, "my milk would be a horrible reminder of the loss and emptiness." But if Lenore lived, she would need my milk and I would like to nurse her if this were possible. I had begged God for help in this decision and decided to say "Yes" to the hope of Lenore's survival. We brought the frozen breast milk to Children's Hospital and the nurses fed it rather than formula to Lenore when she was finally able to drink from a bottle.

After eighteen long days in the hospital Lenore finally came home to us. She still was on Phenobarbital because of some unusual brain-wave activity, but we were able to wean her off of it after about six weeks. The blood from the transfusions turned out to all have been good as well.

To this day we are filled with gratitude and awe of God's grace and love toward us and how he sustained us, of how intimately connected he was with us in our worst hours of pain and suffering. Even though we sometimes felt we were just hanging on to him by our fingernails, he was always there with us. We never know which sufferings will come our way or exactly why they come, but it is deeply true that in our worst sufferings God is *there* helping to carry the cross.

We were also deeply touched by all the blessings showered upon us. Thousands of people in Ohio, Texas, California, New Hampshire, and in Europe — where my family comes from — prayed for Lenore and for us. These prayers, God's mercy, and the five superb sets of doctors and nurses who did all the right things at the right time, saved Lenore.

My mother came from Austria to stay with our other four children through all of this. She cooked for them, got them ready for school, was with them, and loved them. She was an incredible pillar of strength for me. Her help and prayers kept me from collapsing.

Our friends in Steubenville organized two weeks worth of delivered dinners for us after Lenore came home so that I did not have to worry about that part of life after my mother had to go back to Austria. Friends drove our other children home from school so that Michael and I were able to go to Pittsburgh every afternoon.

Without this Christian community of love, prayer, and support, we really could not have survived it all. Our gratitude goes to God, to our family, and to the wonderful friends he sent into our lives who stood with us during this difficult time.

Maria Veronika Healy was born and raised in Innsbruck, Austria, and came to the United States at the age of nineteen. She has a B.A. from the University of Dallas, Texas. She and her husband, Michael, have been married for twenty years and have five children, ages seven through eighteen.

Chapter Ten

Anonymous

Only God Is Constant: A Child's Mental Illness

Ronda: Many mothers suffer with teens and young adults who are deeply disturbed. We tend to feel isolated and like failures. Reading this courageous, open account may help you as it did me.

Here is my story about how God has been faithful to me as a mother, particularly as I have experienced the mental illness of a child.

When I was twenty-two years old I bore my second child, a redhead like her one-year-old sister. A distinguishing fact about her birth was the timing, which I hoped was prophetic. The doctors suggested inducing my labor on October 31, 1974, known to the secular world as Halloween. I declined. Of course, I went into labor while making popcorn balls for trick-or-treaters. While I resisted the trip to the hospital, it became clear that I could not.

Although I had prayed for an All Saints Day delivery, at 11:30 p.m. delivery seemed imminent. Then an odd thing happened. A nurse came in and said, "Oh, it looks like this baby is coming too fast. Can I give you something to slow it down?" "Sure," I replied with a white knuckle grip on the bed rail, and at 12:16 *a.m.* our " little " saint — Catherine — was born. It seemed significant to me that this child was born on All Saints Day, although to this day I cannot explain why.

We were very young parents and lived in a communal setting with other charismatic Catholics. While her older sister was shy, Catherine was outgoing and showy. Infancy was uneventful and normal except that she seemed to be developmentally ahead of herself and even her older sister. We were soon faced with the awkward dilemma of attempting to hold Catherine back so that her sister could catch up. When Catherine was four, she taught herself to read, and from that time on wanted to read, not be read to. She was too independent for that. This was hard for me because it disrupted the bonding time between us that came with story time.

Catherine seemed puzzled by close relationships and responded by withdrawing into books and creative projects. Her artistic side had no limits. She filled our home with drawings, mobiles, needlework, baking, sewed clothes for her stuffed animals, even made holiday decorations for the house that we use to this day. When she entered school, educators raved about her brilliance and that teaching her was a joy. She had the lead in a major play when she was eight, sewed original designs and modeled them for a trophy in 4-H, had a job as a model for Jacobsens', was a preferred baby-sitter by the neighbors, was industrious, helpful, and fun. Although I did not consider myself a "good" mother by nature, I felt that our family life was extremely satisfying and wonderfully fulfilling. It was easy to wrap my self-image around her giftedness. She made *me* look good because she had so many showy gifts.

On the down side, Catherine was moody and restless, and could be annoying to others. Grade school was no problem, but in our Covenant community school she began to be punished for talking out of turn and playing with her pens while the teacher was talking, an impulsive activity that the teacher found bothersome. Looking back, I realize that while Catherine could be a handful, the school standards were too restrictive also.

Corporal punishment was acceptable both in the school and

at our home. Later on, I felt a great deal of guilt about this time in her life. She had an intense interest in pleasing God and was the most spiritual of all my children at that point; however, her desire to please God conflicted with what she saw her peers enjoying. As she grew older, this conflict was very difficult for her.

In tenth grade, she entered the local public high school. Making the transition from a small, narrowly-focused Christian school to a large "anything goes" high school in a liberal city was a huge shock to her system. At first she breezed through with an "A+" average; then she began to falter. Now her illness began to manifest itself. She began to push herself to impossible heights. Although an accomplished seamstress, writer, actress, and pianist, Catherine drove herself to exercise, to develop her singing voice, and to have the most friends of anyone that she knew.

Her obsessions drove her to tears, and she would cry and talk for hours with me about them. I did the usual motherly things to bring her out of herself, and we prayed with her, visited youth-group ministers, and got her involved with disabled children. She cried more and more until I became quite frustrated. She talked about feeling despondent, asked for inner healing prayer, and so we went to a ministry group. Although the prayer and prophecy were insightful, we saw no change.

We moved on to the school counselor when Catherine began to slide academically. His parting words were "This kid is going to need a whole lot more help than I can give her," and I hoped that they were not prophetic. She began writing profanity in big letters on the walls of her bedroom, and we fought a lot. She lost the ability to keep track of time and would wander home hours late after school and wondered why I was upset. At her request, we counseled with a Christian psychologist. After one year and two thousand dollars worth of counseling, we were more confused than ever. Because of her anger level, there was a strong suggestion that at the root of her difficulty was our lack of love and excessive control. There was some truth to this, as our orientation to parenting was authoritative and the community teachings up to that time supported this view.

Unfortunately, our community was dissolving and all the teachings open to attack, and as we began to question everything, we lost our footing for a while. We relaxed our family rules, gave Catherine more space, and tried to understand her more. Soon afterward she began skipping classes and was close to failing in all her subjects, even driver education. Then she stopped coming home after school at all and we were frantic wondering where she was. This began a prolonged series of running-away episodes during which we found that other adults could legally hide her from us to protect her if they felt it was necessary, and because of the stories she told about us, it happened often.

During this highly emotional time, Catherine was starring in the school play *Our Town*. As a sophomore, she was awarded the leading female role traditionally awarded to seniors, and she was brilliant. The play was providential because she had strong motivation to go to rehearsal, and if she failed to come home at night, I could at least find her at school somewhere. She began to talk of suicide during this time and begged to be hospitalized, which we did as soon as the play ended. She was an inpatient at Mercywood Hospital, where she was kept under observation and given medication for depression. We were pulled in for family counseling, and I felt as our family life was on display and then picked apart, sort of like pheasant-under-glass.

We were dismayed to find a host of suspicion and negative input directed at us from the staff and were confused by their questioning. We learned later that Catherine's perspective of our parenting was strongly persecutory and untruthful and yet extremely convincing. So much so that her anger level could be easily connected by an outsider to our abuse of her. Fortunately, we had an excellent psychiatrist who saw what was happening and had different ideas. She concluded that our daughter had a personality disorder and was a compulsive liar. She also felt that her intellect would prove to be a curse as she was able to use her intellect to avoid treatment. I hoped that was not prophetic either.

Two weeks later Catherine was discharged from the

hospital when the insurance money ran out. She had no diagnosis compelling enough to warrant keeping her hospitalized, and no medications had helped her, although there had not been time to give them an adequate trial. Her time at home was intolerable, she refused to continue to take her medication and spent all her time in her room. I found bizarre writing in her room, scores of frantic scribbling on papers thrown everywhere.

After the failed hospitalization attempt she undertook one of her most infamous trips ever. We had a birthday party at our home, and Catherine, as usual, failed to come home from school. Night came but no Catherine. After our guests left, I went up to her room and saw lists on papers strewn on her desk: "Buy black dye, pack and bring stuff to school, get ID, steal car, look around for cash, take bus to Seattle. . . ." I gasped as I realized the horrible truth: My seventeen-year-old daughter had run away and could be anywhere between Michigan and Seattle, Washington. Apparently, Seattle was the Grunge Rock Capital of the USA and she was a "punk" or "death rocker" at the time.

We went immediately to both bus stations in town. One confirmed that a girl dressed in leather with dyed black hair and red eyebrows had boarded a bus to Chicago. Two ideas crashed upon us at once. Not only was her life in serious danger, but she had most certainly forfeited her entire term and would not be able to complete high school.

I was in agony. How could this happen? We were good Christians, had tried to be better than average. We served God, loved him. What did we do wrong? How come bad things happen to good people? I knew I was not the world's gift to motherhood, but I loved my kids the best I could. Wasn't that good enough? How could this be happening to my delightful, precocious, irrepressible redhead? My "A+" gifted student, who had been baptized, confirmed, received the Eucharist, opened her heart to the Holy Spirit?

Catherine was missing and we had to act, but how? It was already dark and she was six hours ahead of us. We had to wait until morning to take action. I began by calling the Chicago Police, runaway shelters, the bus stations, and her friends from school, trying desperately to find clues. The bad news was that the Chicago bus station is in a deserted part of town where pimps and pushers wait to pick up young kids fresh off the bus. It happens to be the runaway capitol of the Midwest. There were hundreds of runaway shelters, bound to confidentiality and to protect her from us, which could not reveal her presence even to her anguished mother. The police were no better. Since Catherine was seventeen, she was no longer a minor and therefore was not eligible to be listed on the national database of runaways. I was informed that she was technically termed "missing voluntary" and was advised to find another kid to love, to let this one go. That was the human solution.

Fortunately, there was the Good News! God stepped into the middle all of this and gave me an inspired word of knowledge to look at two particular streets in Chicago. I got out a map, pinpointed the streets and began calling runaway shelters in that area to see what clues they could give me. I could have shouted when it became clear that this intersection was the epicenter of Chicago's "punk" district: her kind of people! I was so strongly convinced that God had spoken, that we took a trip to Chicago the very next day — Mothers' Day.

Five adults canvassed the Chicago bus station, and as we did, our hearts sank. It was an urban wasteland. Nothing was open, no drug store, fast food eatery, dollar store, nothing. Large gray factories and closed office towers made up the immediate area and as we attempted to trace her footsteps we realized we were ten miles away from the punk district, too far to travel by foot. We tried not to lose hope.

In the punk district we were treated suspiciously because of our age. Although we were wearing all the black clothing we owned, we weren't fooling anybody. We interviewed shopkeepers and showed her photo to whoever looked to be her type and soon got our first break. A proprietor with a maroon Mohawk and multiple piercing recognized her and said she had definitely been there twice the previous day. Not wanting to hope too much, we sought confirmation of this sighting. We got it at a teen night-club. A bouncer had seen her in line and said she was hard not to notice and pretty besides. For the first time in days, I knew that Catherine was alive, and after collecting no more clues, we went home, clinging to our small victory.

Two days later she arrived at our home, clean, rested, and alive. We hugged and cried together, and I tried to talk to her, but she wanted to sleep. As much as I wished to be with her, my husband and I both felt that it was necessary to take her to Mercywood Hospital for observation and drug testing. She was cleared of drug use but was resistant to treatment. They discharged her, unhelped.

Thus began a series of terrifying escapades in which Catherine would be missing for months at a time. Through detective work on my part, I was always able to track her down. It would annoy her, and she would move on if I knew her whereabouts, so I kept my actions covert while I was tracing her. Once again, God was my help as he provided much information. Shortly before her first Christmas on the road, when I was feeling particularly desperate, I received a phone call from a young man named Karl. He told me her whereabouts, address, and work phone and said that after wrestling in prayer himself, he was calling us. She had run away from him and he was as heartbroken as we were.

Another time, a trash company found her license in the trash and called us, alerting us to her residence. A letter arrived in the mail in another instance. It was a subpoena for her to witness stemming from her observation of a felonious assault. Once again we were told whom she was with at the time, and I followed up on that clue. She was picked up twice by the police department. On one occasion, she had stolen a cassette tape and the store prosecuted, which meant many court dates, and visits to a probation officer. Because she missed so many court appointments, we were served a warrant for her arrest, and on one occasion we turned her over to police. This was a dark day for me. Once, I received a letter stating that she had been found by the police in an abandoned building and charged with vagrancy. Over the phone they were able to tell me that at the time they found her, she was confused, malnourished, and said that she had a fever. We asked the police to keep her in jail. Although it seemed so rude to treat her in this fashion, we knew no other way to make sure she received antibiotics, rest, and food. We brought her home after a few days, and after a week, she left again. Because of the cassette theft, Catherine was assigned a probation officer who graciously allowed me to call him and check on her progress. During this time we knew that she was homeless, starving, and completely unreachable by offers of help, outright gifts of money, food, and shelter. One Thanksgiving, after I invited her to dinner and she cursed me for it, I committed her once and for all . . . to the Lord. It was not hard to give her over; we could do nothing to help her. God alone was her protector.

I did several things at this stage that helped save my sanity. I increased my sacramental life, joined a group of women who said the Rosary once a week, and committed myself to meeting with Catherine's' psychiatrist until I understood what happened to this kid. A word about psychiatrists: The wisdom I gained was not spiritual. She was not excessively fond of Catholics and she did not hide it. She made a few jabs at my faith saying things like "Does your 'God' ever let you do something for yourself?" And "Well, there's that Catholic 'guilt' again." Although these comments made me sad that she could not appreciate my faith, I decided not to listen to anything other than psychological wisdom from her; I had other people to support my spirituality. This approach served me so well that even now I marvel at how profoundly helpful the psychological insight has been to my spiritual life and how much a gift knowledge is, even the purely scientific. This relationship was the glue that held me together with the combination of her piercing insight and merciless pointing out of my faults, and her wonderful compassion when I was wounded in battle and confused by my daughter's behavior.

Five months after Thanksgiving, a social worker called to

say that she had Catherine in the emergency room of a major hospital. She told me that my daughter had been brought in agitated and confused and that they had sedated her. The hospital staff sent her by ambulance to a state mental hospital where she was admitted involuntarily by the State of Michigan. God works through the strangest instruments! Although we were not aware of it at the time, the hospital began treating her for schizophrenia. It is clear to me now that many people recognized her psychosis but because of the current confidentiality laws, nobody was allowed to tell us. (This fact in itself is so demoralizing that I could write a whole chapter on it alone!) In fact, she was in the hospital for six weeks before they told us her diagnosis. The next week, they asked if she could come home.

The truth that she was schizophrenic was stunning. We were not prepared for such a major illness. All this time we thought she was simply rebellious to the extreme. Initially, I was disappointed that the fruit of so much prayer and work was going to end with a diagnosis of a major mental illness. But as I prayed, it was clear that God, who had been present throughout our ordeal, was with us now as well, and I was suddenly overwhelmed with joy that we could have a new start. My anger, guilt, and confusion gave way to peace, acceptance, and understanding. As I reviewed the last, chaotic three years, everything was consistent with the diagnosis. She was paranoid, and so she ran away. She was psychotic and her reality was not based on rational thought, hence the tall tales and funny ideas. She was not, after all, a pathological liar: She spoke from *her* reality that was irrational and fear-based. Her refusal to eat although starving was not anorexia nervosa: She had a "thought disorder" which interrupted hunger signals in her brain and never registered in action.

This period of my life was ecstasy! After three years of fearing for her life, my daughter was living comfortably in our home. She lapped up the renewed relationships, and everyone was open to a new beginning. We took lots of field trips together, swam, bowled, shopped. I would tease her and call myself the recreational therapist. She got better every day and soon got a job and finished her high-school education. She tested among the top four percent of all high schoolers in the country at the time, even while receiving heavy doses of drugs and sedatives. Eventually, she improved so much that her medication was changed to a less potent anti-psychotic with fewer side effects and she enrolled in a junior college. She became the family baker and baby-sat for the kids. Her disability was not noticeable to the casual observer.

During this period, ten months from when she first came home, Catherine got a hold of mind-altering drugs at work. We saw a rapid rise of hostility, laziness, lack of appetite, and abnormal sleep patterns. I reported my observations to her social worker, who overlooked them as motherly over-involvement, and she actually encouraged my daughter to move out as a way of solving her problems with her parents. Two months later, my daughter admitted to ceasing her medications and two months after that, her social worker called to report that Catherine was completely delusional and needed an emergency meeting with a psychiatrist. He treated her with handwritten prescriptions and sent her home with us to stabilize her. The message from Social Services was clear: We are not interested in your input; but we want you to be there when we need you to offer practical assistance.

Boy, am I learning fast about why we have so many homeless in our society today! It is this very dynamic that will cause me to become an activist someday. We were not able to stabilize her at home and instead got her into an acute care home for disabled young people where she stabilized so fast that she became their "star" patient and went on to graduate from that home into a less strict group home environment. She began taking control of her life again. She improved her hygiene, restored damaged relationships, and was once again the delightful, fun-loving kid that I used to know.

I wish that I could say that, "All is calm, all is bright," but now, at Christmas time, she is refusing to see us, spitting out her medication, and planning to run away to Seattle. She is frustrating her social-service staff, and clearly Catherine has to decide to cooperate with treatment if she is to get better. My husband and I now take the offensive in prayer every day in the form of praying the Rosary together.

Reading Ronda Chervin's book *The Kiss from the Cross* has kept me focused on the real purpose of trials, and as we have been faced with new trials, we seem to enter deeper into prayer. I have bought five copies of her book and given them to others for Christmas. I find it a most potent weapon in temptation. As I am writing this last paragraph, my daughter turned up in a hospital in Seattle, Washington, after being missing for nine days from her group home. She took a bus there after withdrawing all the money from her account. After falling apart and crying on the parish priest's shoulder, prayers have gone through the parish phone tree and calls are coming through.

It is a hectic time, but in many ways I am dealing with it as a routine disturbance, like wiping up water when the washer overflows. It is inconvenient, fearful, messy, but once it happens the first time, you know what to do. God has shown us that he is involved in this situation and that is all I need to know. He has certainly helped us through a lot, and will continue to do so, although I do not know what form it will take.

Schizophrenia is a disease that affects the patient's ability to love, and ultimately, this is the cruelest part. Because I am easily offended and insecure, this is true penance, perfectly tailored for me. This journey of ours is uncharted and the only constant is God and God alone. For me that will be enough. He will write the end of this story.

The author is a charismatic Catholic — a wife and mother of six.

Chapter Eleven

Shirley Schalk

Not My Mike!
A Child's Accidental Death

*Ronda: I met this beautiful woman at a gathering when she told me her story, I knew it had to be included in **Holding Hands With God**.*

No, no, no, not my Mike . . . the call came at around ten p.m., January 12, 1992 — a car accident, and he wasn't expected to live the night. He was in a coma. Dear God keep him alive till I get there. I screamed, I yelled, I cried. Two of my friends came; we said the Rosary — how could I wait till morning? There were no planes from Florida to Michigan till morning. Oh God, oh God, not Mike.

About three months before the call came, I more than once envisioned a funeral, the church, music, and people. Never did I sense it was going to be my son.

I stayed up all night and went to the airport about four a.m. for a plane that would leave at seven. My flight was a continued cry to God, *keep him alive*. I did pray for his soul. Throughout the night my oldest daughter was at the hospital with Mike reporting to me by phone. I walked in his room; my son was so swollen, tiny nose, slits for eyes. He was unrecognizable. Oh, God, help us. I prayed continuously. This did not seem real. I went through the motions, watching my son shake uncontrollably with no explanation from the doctors as to why.

As I prayed, I sensed my son was afraid. The Lord said a war was going on for Mike's soul and prayer was needed. I asked my friend to call anyone we knew to come to the hospital to pray. She did as I asked, as I told her what I sensed. They all came; some of Mike's young friends were there also.

During the Rosary, God gave me the strength to lean down to my son and say, "Mike don't be afraid, let go and let God finish the plan for your life, whether it is to take you home with him or keep you here with us." Only by the grace of God could I let go, then I'd say, no — *you can make it*. Afterwards, thinking about my back and forth releasing him, I could just hear my son saying, "That's my Mom, can't make up her mind."

During this time, God let his presence be known. My youngest daughter said Mike looked like he was smiling as we watched the swelling go down. A miracle — at five in the morning, thirty-three hours after the accident, I went back in the room and Mike looked completely normal. His face glowed and there was no more shaking or trembling.

We had him transferred by helicopter to another hospital where we thought he'd get better care. Some say people who are in a coma hear. I was told he didn't feel anything, that his head injury was so bad that if he was not in a coma, he could not stand the pain. His leg and arm were broken, and he had one small hole in his forehead.

I was not prepared for his death, even though he was not to survive. He did not die in the thirty-six hours they said he would — hope was there.

He lived one week, Sunday to Sunday in a coma. He went to our Lord at 8:40 p.m., one week and ten minutes after the accident.

I love my son. The morning before he died, I stood by his bed holding his hand. He squeezed my hand, and I said, "Mike, it's Mom. If you hear me, squeeze my hand again" — he did. I often thought it was his good-bye to me. Late that afternoon, his brain started to swell.

Sunday morning I asked the attendant to please leave me alone with my son. The Mass was on TV and I wanted to share the Mass with my son, believing he could hear. I read Scripture to him. Five different priests came at different times, and he was anointed by them.

Prayer was constant — Divine Mercy devotion, the Rosary — we even sang. Mike loved taking pictures and having his picture taken, and we put them around the room. He had so many friends. As I said, I wasn't prepared for his dying, and when he did, and the doctor told us, life went out of me. We stood around Mike's bed and sang and prayed him into Jesus' welcoming hands and heart. I prayed for Mike's healing. God answered that prayer. It was clear that Mike said yes to Jesus and our Lord gave him the ultimate healing — life eternal. The presence of God was all around Mike and us.

That was January, 1992. I miss him so very much. The great mercy of God keeps me going. He allows me comforts such as Holy Thursday in 1992. I gazed at the heavens, my heart bursting, and in the heavens appeared beautiful colors and the Sacred Heart of Jesus and Mary. I said, "Thank you Lord, thank you, but (just like a Mother) could I just have a glance of Mike?"

Again, in his great Mercy, I saw my son standing in white below to the right of Jesus with many little children. Oh how good God is.

Two months after Michael's death, I was back in Florida in my own parish for the first time. I began to sob, and as I closed my eyes a vision came. Our altar became the throne of God, and at the feet of the throne, many angels were praising God, and in the middle a little to the left stood my son as he looked when he was seventeen.

From time to time, mostly at Mass, the Lord allows a brush of a kiss on my cheek. I feel especially close to Michael at Mass.

Thank you, Lord, for leading me into the Catholic faith. Without the faith I embraced and love, I could not stand that my child died.

Our Lord told me in 1984, at a time I had concern for the life style Mike and many young people were experiencing, that by my son's conversion many souls would be touched. I held onto that, not aware that this would come to pass by Michael's death and new eternal life. One experience — one of Mike's many close friends was out of state and could not get home for the services. He said he had what he thought was a spiritual experience. A great bright light appeared and then Mike was standing there and he (Mike) said "It's OK, Gus, it's OK." This event is being repeated among Michael's friends.

The word God gave to me — came to pass. Hearing this experience helped and gave me strength. I began to heal somewhat in this deep, deep agony of separation by death with hope my soul will be worthy to live eternally with God the Father, Jesus his Son, Mary our Mother, and unite with Michael, Mike, Mikie my beloved son that Jesus loaned to me and now has in his total care — no sorrow, no pain, just the love of God Eternal.

To other mothers who have children separated from us by death . . . I say . . . have hope . . . there is a time coming when we will see them again. They are gone from here (earth) but not lost.

God be merciful to all parents.

Shirley Schalk is a mother in the Hearts of Healing Ministry.

Chapter Twelve

Carol McCormick

We Named Her Catherine-Rose: A Small Child's Death

Ronda: Early miscarriages are so common that some women rarely talk of them, especially if they have other children. The death of a newborn is especially painful, but as in all the stories in this book, there is consolation in the Lord.

Catherine-Rose.
"She was just a preemie," someone said to my mother.
I was shocked.
"Just" a preemie!
How could anyone be so cruel?
She was not just a preemie. She was my baby. My Catherine, my Catherine-Rose.

My husband, John, and I had gone to the regular monthly appointment with our midwife, Patty Lee. She was a wonderful woman who answered our questions patiently and thoroughly. That day, July second, 1992, I told her of an increased vaginal discharge. I hadn't thought much of it.

John and I had been married three years and had been trying to have a baby ever since. A doctor had told me that I didn't ovulate and he held little hope for us to conceive without medical help, yet here I was in the fifth month! Everything was going smoothly. My delivery date was October thirty-first but I always said it was November first, All Saints Day. How prophetic.

Patty said she wanted to do an internal exam just to make sure everything was OK.

I'll never forget what she said next.

"Carol, you're three to four centimeters dilated and your membranes are bulging."

"What!?" I cried, "that's not right! They're not supposed to be like that, are they?"

John took my hand. I started to cry.

Patty asked if I had felt any contractions.

I told her I had felt nothing.

I immediately blamed myself. It was all the work I had done in the garden. The walking. The teaching.

Patty assured me that some women do high-impact aerobics during pregnancy and are fine. It wasn't my fault.

John kept trying to console me.

All I knew was that my baby was in terrible danger.

We'd tried to conceive for so long and now this. Why?

Patty explained something about incompetent cervix. Some women's cervixes are not strong enough to hold the weight of a baby and they open up without contractions. She thought that this might be what happened.

An ambulance was called. I was rushed to Reading Hospital and Medical Center.

The first doctor that I saw had a very chauvinistic attitude. He mentioned something about doing an amniocentesis and if the baby was not "normal" he wouldn't try so hard to save it. I told him an amniocentesis would not be necessary and he'd better try to save my baby.

By this time I was having regular uterine contractions and was given shots of tributiline in an attempt to stop them.

Tributiline makes your heart race. I felt like I had just run a marathon.

The nurses wheeled in an ultrasound machine and I saw her. She was bouncing up and down as she had on all the ultrasounds. "My little gymnast" I used to call her.

When I had come home from Birthright five months before after finding out I was pregnant, I eagerly waited for John to come home from work. When he did I said, "Hi Daddy." At first it didn't register then he exclaimed, "It was positive?!" He bounded up the stairs, picked me up and hugged me. "Oh, I don't want to hurt you!" He put me down. He knelt next to me and talked to the baby inside my womb. He put his big hands gently on my abdomen and prayed to God for this little one. We thanked him for so great a gift: our love had become flesh. This was the first of many times that we prayed over our little one. Each night John would put his hand on my stomach and we'd pray that he/she would follow Jesus all his/her life. Then he would talk to the baby. "Hey baby! This is your Daddy speaking!" We would laugh and talk of all our plans for the person growing inside me.

I started a little book for her. In the book I would write important events in the life of this newest McCormick: "Dear baby, we saw your picture today for the first time . . . we heard your heart beating . . . Daddy loves you . . . we can't wait to see you!"

Each month we would go to our appointment at the Reading Birth and Women's Center. Patty never rushed us. The center's emphasis was on education. There was a large lending library and time was spent during each appointment explaining various things about pregnancy and fetal development. Good nutrition and exercise were a must, and patients took responsibility for their prenatal care. I weighed myself, read my sugar and acetone levels and marked these on my chart. We were encouraged to read our charts.

Suddenly, all that changed.

As soon as I got to the hospital, Patty was no longer allowed to be my primary caretaker. She had gone to school for eight years. She had delivered more babies than most doctors and certainly more than the resident that ended up delivering my baby. Midwives stay with you, support you, from the time you start labor until the baby is born. They don't step in at the last moment, cut your perineum to hurry things up, catch the baby, then send you a whopping bill. They give you choices. You want to walk around during labor? Fine. You want to have the baby in a full size bed instead of one where you feel like your butt is going to fall off? Fine. You don't want to be in that degrading position with your feet up in stirrups? (This is childbirth, not horseback riding, isn't it?)

I hope that in the very near future midwives will be on the staff of every hospital so that those of us with high-risk pregnancies can have the high-tech equipment we may need and the warm and competent hand that we want.

There I was, in the last place I ever wanted to be: a cold, sterile hospital. A belt was strapped around my waist to monitor uterine activity. The wires from it fed into a machine which showed a pen writing on a graph. I was obsessed with watching this pen move up and down as my belly tightened and loosened with each contraction. I finally turned to lie facing away from it. The tributiline wasn't doing any good. All those "mountains" on the graph showed it. My body was in labor, my baby would be born, and at twenty-two weeks she would surely die. When she is born what do we do? Do we send her to the neonatal intensive care unit (NICU) and have them try to save her or do we let her die peacefully in our arms?

John was finishing up his M.A. in theology. He'd taken plenty of moral courses. I had taken "Issues in Reproductive Technology" at Franciscan University of Steubenville. We had discussed the issues: contraception, abortion, euthanasia, test-tube babies. We knew where we stood: firmly within the wisdom of the Catholic Church. But now it was more than an issue to be discussed: This was our baby.

Two perinatologists — specialists in maternal-fetal medicine — five residents, and our midwife said that the baby would almost surely die if she was born now. They normally don't even try to save babies before twenty-four weeks gestation unless the parents insist.

We were cautious.

"Do you mean the baby would be retarded?" we asked. We'd tried to adopt a special-needs child the year before. We were certainly willing to care for this little one. We agonized back and forth. The doctors explained that she had very little (if any) lung tissue and the force of the respirator would destroy it. We wanted her to live so badly.

If she were born right now she would only have a one-percent chance of survival, but as each week went by the percentage would increase so that at twenty-eight weeks she would have a ninety percent chance of making it. The key was to keep her safely inside of me until at least twenty-eight weeks.

We tried a stronger drug in a further attempt to stop labor: magnesium sulfate.

Magnesium sulfate goes into your veins like fire. The nurses hung two bags: one with the drug and one with water. The water keeps the magnesium sulfate from burning up your veins. The idea is for it to shut your uterus down and keep it from contracting. Unfortunately it can also shut your lungs and other vital organs down too. Because of this, the nurses hooked a blood pressure cuff to my arm which took my blood pressure every fifteen minutes. Someone came in to check my reflexes and vital signs on a regular basis too. These things start to go before the major organs. I was in the Trendelenburg position (head down, feet up) to keep the pressure off my cervix in an attempt to keep it from opening any further. My stomach kept twisting and I would retch again and again until there was nothing left. The magnesium sulfate made me sweat profusely.

I felt a bit like Christ on the cross. I was his body. The IVs and the needles were the nails they drove into his hands and feet. The bed was the wood. I was on fire from the magnesium sulfate, delirious with its potency. The blood pressure cuff kept going off and keeping me awake and someone kept banging on my knees to make sure I was staying alive. I kept thinking of Jesus. "Father, take this cup away from me!" His mind was tortured. My mind was tortured. The physical pain was nothing compared to the psychological and emotional pain of knowing that my body was pushing my baby out before she was ready. I felt like a murderer. I wished there was a crucifix on the wall. I united my pain with his. If only she would live it would all be worth it.

John's Mom and Dad came. They prayed with us. Mom read Psalm 91, "You who dwell in the shelter of the Most High, who abide in the shadow of the Almighty, will say to the Lord, 'My refuge and my fortress, my God in whom I trust.'"

Patty Lee and a perinatologist came in. They spoke with us again about what would happen if the baby was born soon. The chances she had of living. Should she go to the NICU or should we hold her and let her die in our arms?

Finally Patty said emphatically, "Carol, if this baby's born now she'll be blind, deaf, and never have bowel and bladder control — if she survives at all!"

The weight of it came crushing down on me. Tears streamed down my face. "It would be better for her to be in Jesus' arms than mine if she's going to suffer so much."

That's when we decided that it would be more cruel, indeed selfish of us, to try to make her live if God was calling her home to himself.

John spent the night on a blanket on the floor next to my bed. His silent strength, the depth of his love, was incredible. It got me through the hell we were going through and the pain of the weeks and months to follow. His love and our faith are the greatest gifts of my life.

Sometime in the middle of the night I heard someone say that the contractions were slowing down. I was so relieved. There was hope.

The next day, Friday, July third, the McCormicks came again.

We prayed. The magnesium sulfate continued to course through my veins with its fire. The contractions had stopped. "Thank God. We're in the clear," we thought.

At times the nurses would come in to listen to the baby's heartbeat with their special stethoscope. Then they would let me listen. I felt so one with her. Only I could hear her heart beat at that moment. I would listen to the fast gallop of her tiny heart with my eyes closed, willing it to keep going, to keep beating. "Stay inside of Mommy little baby. Stay safe and warm inside me till the time is right to be born."

I am so grateful to the nurses at Reading Hospital for encouraging me to listen to her heartbeat.

The day wore on. I chewed on ice chips, threw up. Doctors and nurses came in and out asking questions, the lady in the next bed talked on the phone for what seemed hours at a time. Somebody kept banging on my ankles and knees to make sure I still had reflexes. The blood pressure cuff kept squeezing my left arm and that damn magnesium sulfate kept pouring into the veins in my right arm.

The nurses were in and out rearranging the pillows, mopping my forehead, and trying to encourage us. Amid the needles and tubes, the sterile hospital procedures, and the gruffness of some of the residents, the nurses were the hands and hearts that made it human.

When the nurses next wheeled the ultrasound machine in, our little gymnast wasn't jumping up and down. She was lying very still. The magnesium sulfate had gotten to her and had quieted her down. Her heart was still beating, though. Later I felt some water leak out. I thought that it was from the Foley Catheter they had inserted to empty my bladder. Mom McCormick knew better. A doctor did an internal exam. He looked up at me.

"Carol. Your cervix is fully dilated. I could feel the baby's foot."

All I could think of was, "Oh my God! We stopped the contractions and it meant nothing! The cervix opened up anyway . . . why, God? Why?"

I asked him what we were to do next.

"I'll have to stop the magnesium sulfate. It's not doing any good," he said.

"Then what?"

"You'll go into labor."

"Then she'll be born. Then she'll die," I thought to myself.

I was switched to a labor room. Soon after the magnesium sulfate was stopped I started having strong contractions. The nurses gave me something for the pain which put my brain into a fog. Suddenly I felt an irresistible urge to push. I wanted so badly to keep her inside, to keep her warm and safe. She belonged in my womb, yet my body was rejecting her. She was born in five or six pushes — feet first. The doctor put her immediately in my arms.

She was beautiful.

She looked just like John when he's asleep but so tiny! She weighed one pound, three-and-a-half ounces and was thirteen-and-one-half inches long. Like a little doll.

We baptized her. John said those great words, "I baptize you, Catherine-Rose, in the name of the Father, and of the Son, and of the Holy Spirit." Our saint.

The nurses put her in a little pink dress with a pink ribbon then brought her back and put her in my arms.

She blinked a few times and yawned.

I kept looking at her. Wanting to imprint all her little features on my mind. I did not want to forget. Her eyes and nose were like John's, her mouth like mine. She had a lot of what would have become hair. Her hands were so tiny. "Remember every detail," I kept telling myself, "every bit of her."

The nurses had taken a picture in the NICU and now I asked them to take more. They took some with Catherine alone and some with the three of us. She didn't look as good in the pictures as she did in real life. I guess photography just can't capture what the human heart sees in someone it loves.

To us she was beautiful. We all took turns holding her. We kept telling her how much we loved her.

The force of the love I was feeling was overwhelming, I had never felt any thing like it. The love of a mother for her child. It was like a tidal wave breaking across my whole being. My heart was bursting with love for this child. An intensity of love I'd never known or felt before.

I told her I was sorry over and over again, that my body made her be born too early.

Later there were those who said, "Perhaps something would have been wrong with her. It was for the best."

Nothing was wrong with her. My cervix was incompetent. What a horrible thing to say anyway: "It's for the best that your baby died."

People said such stupid things. They tried to give us pat answers. Quick fixes. It is like trying to put a Band-Aid on a huge, gaping wound.

"You're young, you'll have another."

I wanted to say, "Will another one replace my Catherine?"

I realize that people are very uncomfortable in these situations, but to say something that minimizes the pain is the worst thing that you can do.

Cry with us if you can. Hold us. But don't minimize the pain with some trite little saying.

There is nothing that can be said.

Friends would try to comfort me that Catherine was in heaven and we were the most successful of parents.

I want her here with me, I would cry. I want to hold her in my arms, change her diaper, sing to her at night. I long to see her in her Daddy's strong arms in a frilly pink dress with a bonnet framing the little face that had her Daddy's eyes.

My heart still aches that she was buried without a bonnet. I know that the real "her" is not in the grave, but I am her mother. I was in charge of her body. She should have had a bonnet to keep her head warm in that cold, cold earth.

C. S. Lewis in his *A Grief Observed* speaks of a mother's grieving:

> "If a mother is mourning not for what she has lost but for what her dead child has lost, it is a comfort to believe that the child has not lost the end for which it was created . . . A comfort to the God-aimed eternal spirit within her. But not to her motherhood. This specifically maternal happiness must be written off. Never, in any place or time, will she have her son on her knees, or bathe him, or tell him a bedtime story, or plan for his future, or see her grandchild" (page 30).

Yes I'm glad she's in heaven but I'm not glad that she's not here. Mother comes from the word matter and is tied inextricably with it. Didn't Jesus take on human flesh in the womb of a woman? The material, the physical, is good.

One of my dearest friends lost two little boys in miscarriages. Her daughters believe that their brothers are "growing up in heaven" and, since Catherine is younger than they are, that the boys are caring for her. This may be true, but I hope God keeps her a baby for me. I hope that some day I will be able to care for her. I dream that I will be on my way into the Celestial City and Our Lady will come to meet me. There will be a tiny bundle in her arms. She will hand it to me and inside will be my little girl. She will still be a baby and I will care for her the way I wanted to on this earth.

Enough of dreams.

The doctor came in periodically to check her heart rate.

It kept dropping.

120 beats per minute . . . 80 . . . 40 . . . 20 . . .

Why?

I don't know if it was the pain killer that I was given just before delivery or the shock and inability to handle the reality of what was happening, but I was very much out of it.

Numb.

I wished I could shake myself and wake up because I knew these were the only moments I would have with her.

The doctor came in again and told us that her heart rate was four beats per minute.

John was holding her a few minutes later when the doctor came in again.

He put the stethoscope to her chest and listened.

"I'm sorry.

"There is no heartbeat.

"Your daughter is dead."

These words are imprinted in my brain. I used to wake up in the night and hear them over and over again. "I'm sorry. There is no heart beat. Your daughter is dead."

John came to me. He put her in my arms.

I think we cried.

In the days that followed we bought a casket for her, chose a plot of ground and flowers. We were twenty eight years old.

These are things that older people do.

It seemed so unreal. I felt like I was in a daze.

My milk came in. My breasts were full. There was no baby to nurse.

The evening before the funeral I was upstairs trying to rest. On the table next to the bed was a bottle of pain pills. I reached over to take them all. To fall asleep forever. As my hand clasped the bottle, a flood of anger filled my brain. I flung the bottle across the room.

"The devil will not win!" I thought.

Catherine is with Jesus. I want to be with her someday. I could not do that to John. She was his daughter too. I would not have him lose both of us at once.

How could I have thought of suicide?

I was a good Catholic. I had been a postulant in Mother Teresa's Missionaries of Charity before I realized my vocation was to be a wife and mother. My faith had always been important to me.

John and I walked up the aisle at the funeral Mass the next

day. He carried the casket with her body in it and laid it in front of the altar.

"The box is too small," our seven-year-old niece had said. She had been to other funerals. She knew the box should be bigger.

The priest said the Mass of the Angels. At one point he prayed a very beautiful prayer: "May the angels lead you into paradise. May the martyrs welcome you and take you to the Holy City, the new and eternal Jerusalem."

It was a comfort to me to hear the familiar words I had sung when I was in the convent.

I had prayed that my children would be saints. I even had the audacity to pray that I would be one. Now I could see that God was a huge, raging fire, drawing me closer with whispered words of love only to burn me when I got too close.

Was there a God?

How could there be, with this much pain in my heart?

There is none. A void. That's all. We're all like madman running around with no sense. No rhyme or reason.

I wrote about these things and others in my journal and in the baby's book I had started. It helped to get my jumbled up thoughts and feelings out of my head and down on paper.

July 4th, 1992

My Dearest Baby.

My Dearest Catherine-Rose, you're not in my womb anymore. . . . I'm so empty now. So empty. . . . Your little eyes were closed but they were Daddy's eyes. . . . Your nose was his and your feet, so big. Oh Jesus, why did you take my baby? Why?

Last night she was born and this morning she slipped away.

July 7th

Catherine-Rose, will you still call me Mommy?

July 12th

There has been no suffering like this suffering.

113

Holding Hands With God

No pain like this pain.
A mother's heart.
A mother's empty arms.
Empty womb.
Broken heart.

July 15th

My heart is filled with a grief I cannot bear. If people only knew how hard it is to pack away my maternity clothes. To be looking for a job in the fall.

I wanted to be home with my baby in the fall.

I wrote poems for her.

The child beyond my grasp now
Once played within my womb
She who danced and swam inside me
Now lies inside a tomb
A merciless judge has slain me
rent my heart in two
tore her from my loving arms
and pierced me through and through
Why does He give,
to take away?
Give joy,
then pain to follow?
What God, what Father
Would give joy, full and fruitful,
pregnant with life,
To strip it away, leaving
death and pain,
emptiness and barrenness?
Who can know the heart of a mother
Her sacrifice, her gift of self
Her joys and love unbounding?
Who knows her pain,
deep and piercing?

Only the one whose heart was also pierced
She who stood at the foot of the Cross
Her dying Son spread out there
His love unfurled and nailed
Her Mother's heart breaking
My Mother, my Queen.

I took refuge in the Mother of Sorrows even as I pushed God farther and farther away. She was near, but he was awful and omnipotent and cruel. A letter from Sister Patrice and the Franciscans Sisters, TOR, helped me a great deal.

"Our Lady who is the Mother of Sorrows also understands your deep pain as she held the dead body of her Son so close to herself. May she also support and hold you close to herself and comfort you. So many times I am aware that we do not live for this world. I often tell Jesus that he alone is my heaven. . . ."

At first I thought there must not be a God at all. I reasoned that if God is all-powerful, he could have stopped the labor and he didn't. So either he couldn't or he wouldn't. If he couldn't then he's some sort of weakling and not God at all. If he wouldn't than how could he be loving?

I vacillated between clinging to my faith like a man does to a lifeboat in the middle of a churning sea and throwing it to the wind. For example:

July 14th

My only refuge is the Heart of Jesus where the fires burn so hot, fires of love.

The passion of God.

My heart is on fire with this sorrow. Consumed and crying. Pain. A crucible. A dying inside.

July 30th

Is God a sadistic puppeteer looking down upon us? Would it not be a sadistic sort of god who would send us screaming through these horrible circumstances, watching us writhing in pain, only to condescend to help us again? If he does exist, he is not the sort of god anyone would want to get to know, the kind you hear is faithful, loving, and kind. He seems more like the wrathful pagan gods.

I told my spiritual director of ten years that I had no faith. I must have never had it. He said he had no answers. He said faith isn't faith until there are no answers, until you can say, "I don't understand, this makes no sense. God knows. That is enough." "Faith isn't faith until you're leaning so completely on it that if it moves you'll fall."

Weeks turned into months. John and I promised each other that if one of us woke up in the night crying we would wake the other up so that we could hold each other. So we wouldn't cry alone.

We watched a lot of TV just to forget the pain for a while.

I kept looking for a book to read, a person to call, something, *anything* that would take the suffering, the stone in my heart, away for even a little while. I realized, as C.S. Lewis did after losing his wife, that there was no way around it. Only through it.

> ". . . Aren't all these notes the senseless writhing of a man who won't accept the fact that there is nothing we can do with suffering except to suffer it? Who still thinks there is some device (if only he could find it) which will make pain not to be pain. It doesn't really matter whether you grip the arms of the dentist's chair or let your hands lie in your lap. The drill drills on" (*A Grief Observed*, page 38).

I called my spiritual director. "I still can't pray," I told him, "I can't sit by myself and try to concentrate or I cry."

"How dare you say that your tears are not prayers! Grieving is a prayer. Your suffering is joined to Jesus. Your tears are mingled with his." He said that it's important to not get over the grieving too soon. That now I'm grieving for myself and not for Catherine which is OK.

We went to a support group for parents whose children have died called The Compassionate Friends. They were fantastic. To hear their stories, how they coped with death, gave us hope that we could keep going. Keep living.

There have been a few "breakthroughs," times when the weight on my heart was lifted and a shaft of light broke through. One was a tape by Father Pavich (from Medjugorje). He spoke of how the word "persevere" means to "go through difficulties." He said we have to go past the joyful mysteries and into the sorrowful. Satan would have us believe that God has abandoned us. We must say, "Abba Father, into your hands I commend my spirit," from the cross.

There could be no Easter Sunday without Good Friday.

Another time I was at a prayer meeting when I heard these words as if for the first time:

"I am the resurrection and the life. He who believes in me will never die. I will raise him up on the last day."

Yes. He is life. Death has no power over the Christian.

"There will be no mourning, no crying, no pain or death anymore. Alleluia!"

A breakthrough in my seeking to understand why God would allow pain was found in a poem by Francis Thompson called *The Hound of Heaven*.

". . . All of which I took from thee I did but take,
Not for thy harms,
But just that thou might'st seek it in my arms.
All of which thy child's mistake
Fancies lost, I have stored for thee at home:
Rise, clasp my hand, and come!"

It is not because he is a mean and wrathful pagan god that he sends us difficulties. It is because he wants us to turn to him, to come into his arms, and let him love us back to life. I realized that the house of my faith had been weak and tottering. Through

Catherine's death I was stripped down to nothing so he could build up a new and stronger faith in me.

Two and a half years after Catherine died another significant moment of grace occurred.

I was reading the story of the daughter of Jairus in Mark's Gospel, chapter five, verses 21-24 and 35-43.

"Your daughter is dead," it says in verse thirty-five. I had not realized that line was in there. It was spoken to Jairus the synagogue official who had come to ask Jesus to heal his daughter. Those words were also spoken to John and me, "I'm sorry, there is no heartbeat. Your daughter is dead." I'd heard them reverberate in my brain a hundred times. Jesus said to the official, "Fear is useless, what is needed is trust." That is what he said to me in that moment, "Fear is *useless*, what is needed, my daughter, is *trust*."

"Trust that she is in my care. Trust that I (God) knew what I was doing when I took her from you and brought her home. Appearances are deceiving. She is living. She is living."

Surrender.

Only surrender brings peace.

Jairus' daughter opened up her eyes to see the face of Jesus. Though Jesus did not raise Catherine-Rose in this life, no doubt she opened her eyes, on the other side, to gaze into his beautiful eyes. Even now our rose lifts her face up to Jesus, up to God, basking in the Father's love. Our little bud never blossomed on earth, she's blooming in heaven under Mary's tender care, in the Father's house: loving, singing, happy.

So in the end Mary led me back to Jesus.

It has been very difficult to write these memoirs.

I was hesitant to begin because I hated the thought of my heart bleeding all over the pages for everyone to see. I did it first and most importantly to honor her. To fulfill, a little bit, that maternal need that a dead child not be forgotten. Secondly, I wrote for all those who are friends and family to parents who have lost children. In hope that you might gain understanding in how to comfort the grieving. Especially in knowing what to say and what not to say. Thirdly, this is for all those whose hearts are crying and whose arms are empty. May God comfort you and hold you.

Soon after Catherine's death a wise physician told us, "There's never a perfect time to have a baby — start trying right away!" At first we were afraid of going through the same thing again, but in three months we conceived. Joseph Leo John was born one year, almost to the day, after Catherine-Rose was buried. One child can never replace another but Joseph has brought us a deep joy and a courage to hope again.

Carol McCormick, wife of John McCormick, is an at-home mom of Joseph, and newborn Benedictus and a member of the Secular Franciscan Order.

Chapter Thirteen

Ronda Chervin

God Welcomed Him Home: A Young Man's Suicide

Ronda: In 1991, my nineteen-year-old son, an excellent student, promising composer of classical music, and deeply spiritual young man, committed suicide. The grief made me so miserable and numb I could never think of writing about this tragic event. However, being a writer by trade, I came to see that only by wrapping my emotions in words could I come to grips with them and trace the way God's grace came to meet me in that awful darkness.

On February 21, 1991 we received this letter from our son. It was mailed from Big Sur, a beautiful area high above the Pacific on the California coast.

> Dear Family,
> I have discovered that the fathomless currents of my soul which once overflowed within me to give me new life have now flowed past the green valleys and mountains, which are purpose and hope, and have reached the sea, which is death. The very force within me which hitherto brought me rebirth and a glorious bubble of dreams, now

turns backwards towards destruction since the vanquishment of all that gave joy and savor to life. When I see the incredible beauty of waterfalls, rivers, forests, and oceans my spirit knows that the life force is long gone and that the roads I once traveled by can never be walked again, and hope was a bittersweet dream of the past, and the only pure, beautiful road that nature opens is a fall toward my friend, the end.

Father, you must understand you are in no way to blame for the course of events. If it were not for the fact that I have slipped beyond the salvations of humanity, your efforts would have done miraculous wonders to help me. My life is your life and yours is mine and many a time have we given each other light in the darkness. Yet how could you possibly help me when I have known, yes I know beyond doubt that my cycle is over and all I can do is walk towards the darkness, which is the end. I know this so deeply that none can save me. Better that I am free to pursue my destiny with beauty and integrity than to allow that other men or institutions take over and pretend to protect me from what will always be so. I have searched all my life and found "nothing" on the top of Mount Carmel. It is as true and natural as the dust from which we came.

God has been good to me, for I have found the most beautiful country in all the world on which to lay my head. Just north of Andrew Molera State Park and Point Sur there is an enormous arched bridge. A rainbow bridge which spans a quiet valley in which there lies a green meadow covered with yellow flowers surrounding a river which runs through the birch trees then curves to make its way through a land of green ivy then swirls through the sand to make a final passage to the sea. I will land in the green meadow then perhaps be carried to the ocean if I am lucky. I can imagine no more beautiful and perfect way to witness the end of time.

These final days spent in nature and at the monastery have purified my soul and given me peace for my departure. Considering myself, I realize that it is right that I should die as a child still within sight of my youth and all of the wonders, and treasures, and creations, and laughter, and songs which make up Charlie, yet will be no more. I am not sad that I never became a man because if I look even fleetingly at the possibilities of the future I feel only dread and loathing. I am the King of the Past. In my kingdom I have experienced all the love and fulfillment and colors and dimensions that a person can hope for. I see no cause for grief. As a free spirit, wanderer and pilot of my destiny, I cry to all of you, you that I love . . . .

> FAREWELL!
> Charlie Chervin

We read the letter and became frantic.

But then, he called once more. "Hello. I'm filling the car up with gas. On my way."

My husband, Martin, was stunned. When he told Charlie that he had gotten the suicide letter, Charlie said, "Oh, no!" as casually as if it were a broken social engagement. In a state of incredible fear, my husband begged him to go back to the monastery and wait for him to arrive. He agreed. Martin said we would not call the police if he waited for us.

But we did feel we had to call the police. They say they planted one squad car at the monastery and one at the bridge he described in his note. They told us to stay home in case he was headed our way.

I couldn't stand it. I left Martin home with the family and decided I would fly up to San Jose. The earliest flight I could get would land in time to get to Big Sur and drive back with Charlie once they found him.

"Out of the depths I cry to thee" (Ps 130). All the way I prayed incessantly, mostly cries of Jesus, Jesus, Jesus — or Rosary prayers over and over and over again. I rode to the airport with my Diana's husband, Pete; somehow at the very hour he had done it we were still talking about bluffing. I am sure you have heard the theory that those who leave notes around to let you know "before" are really just crying out for help by means of the threat.

Happily my husband had not wanted me to travel alone. He asked my sister's husband, Arthur Eaton, who lives in Berkeley if he would meet me at the San Jose airport and drive me down to Big Sur.

Arthur is a psychologist. He married my sister, also a convert, now a sacred dancer, after being married before. He is an Episcopalian. In the past I had not gotten along too well with him. He is very life-loving and intuitive, whereas I am a crusader type who likes to debate matters vehemently and syllogistically. This situation brought out all his most lovable and wise qualities, and he became one of the comforts that came out of the whole miserable tragedy.

The ride from San Jose to Big Sur took a very long time. On the way we kept stopping at phone booths so I could call home to see if the police had intercepted Charlie. Most of the time we did not talk about what would happen if he had done it, but rather what kind of family therapy might be helpful after we caught up with him.

I had made a reservation at a motel right near the monastery since it might be closed for the night by the time we got there. About an hour away from Big Sur we stopped at a large motel with a bar to make another call. They told us that the little motel near the monastery closed up by nine and we should stay with them. Frustrated, I decided to put in a call to the local police before retiring.

"Hello, this is Mrs. Chervin, the one whose son Charles you are looking for. Did you find him yet?"

"Wait a minute. Give us your number and the detective will call you back."

Rock music banging away from the bar, I waited for the call.

"Are you Mrs. Chervin?"

"Yes."

"Oh, that one! He jumped. He's dead! Do you mind if we ask you a few questions?"

By that time Arthur had grabbed hold of me. No, I didn't want them to call my husband. I would do it. Then they could call me back with their fifty questions. Later I wrote a letter to the detective telling him that because I read lots of mystery stories I understood that they had to get to the questions right away. How do they know I'm the mother and not someone who pushed him off and wanted to know if he survived or not? But since ninety percent of the time the caller is probably the real mother, couldn't they break the news a little more comfortingly?

The cashier started to notice that I was crying and making phone call after phone call. "Excuse me," she said. "I couldn't help overhearing. It happens that the paramedic who went down to get your son is at the bar. He would like to talk to you if you can stand it."

A big, burly guy came over. Gently he told me that he had been summoned just minutes after Charlie jumped. A hitchhiker had witnessed the leap, thinking before that Charlie was just enjoying the view from the bridge. The last minute he ran back to his truck and brought a blanket — for protection against injuries? For comfort? It was not the large rainbow bridge in the suicide note, but a smaller one. This paramedic's volunteer work is to get down the 170 feet on the rope, try to revive the suicide, and bring the victim up with him on the rope to the ambulance.

He said that Charlie had no pain or wounds. The internal

organs tend to give out on the way down. He had landed on his feet. He could not be revived.

Reluctantly the police said they would postpone the autopsy until I could see him at the mortuary next morning early. Arthur called my twin sister who arranged an early flight into Monterey the next day. I think he knew that it would take the bottle of wine he bought to give me the freedom to let out all the screaming misery right away in the safety of his company in the double motel room.

Finally I was able to sleep, setting the alarm for 5:30 a.m. to make it to the airport to pick up my sister and then to the mortuary before the autopsy crew beat me to him.

It was very good to see my sister. She had loved my son very much and identified with him as a fellow artist: a dancer who understood the life of a musician in a way different from the rest of the family. We got to the mortuary. They told me that he was in a body-bag and we could only see his head. At that point I thought the whole family would drive up and we would have a funeral Mass in a church in Monterey. My daughter Diana was especially anxious to make the trip and be close to me in my ordeal. Arthur went out to make the arrangements for a hotel near the church. My sister Carla De Sola went in with me to the room where I would see the body of Charlie.

All through the night I had been identifying this encounter with the Pietà. Like Mary, I was going to hold my dead son in my arms, and she would be there to help me through it.

Up to this time I had only seen the dead bodies of loved ones embalmed in open coffins at funerals. I had been horrified by the way they looked with their distorted smiles or other unrecognizable features. This was altogether different.

Charlie looked beautiful! His face looked solemn and somehow focused. Of course, as I now find is quite common, I had fantasies of resurrecting him. I kissed his cool forehead and his heavy, wet brown hair and prayed while laying relics of Saint Catherine of Siena and Conchita on his head. My sister laid the cross she had received at Baptism on him, and did a slow dance around his body. I kissed him one last time saying, "Goodbye, sweet prince."

Soon they were ushering us out to lead in the autopsy people. Later I requested and received a clump of his hair which I sewed into material from the kimono my mother wore at my birth. This little pouch I pin into my bra where it nestles in the space from the mastectomy I had the year before this. I since learned that it used to be the custom to put the hair of the dead into locket-brooches to be worn by the surviving women of the family.

I was happy to learn that Charlie had placed an indication on his driving license for donation of his organs. The people running the organ donation were extremely kind and sympathetic as they got my added permission.

My husband wanted Charlie cremated, so that was all arranged. What was left was to take the long drive to the monastery to retrieve his pickup truck and try to get it sold. Halfway there, I decided it was too much to try to deal with a used-car salesman on top of everything else. My husband absolutely never wanted to see this getaway truck again. So I donated it to the monastery.

It was the beginning of comfort to receive Holy Communion at the astoundingly holy chapel of the monks. It turned out several of them were men I had known before. The monks said that he had been so quiet they didn't get to know Charlie at all. He seemed to blend so well with their atmosphere they wondered if he had a vocation. It would have been good if I had told them about his state of mind on arrival since, in fact, many would-be suicides looking, as Charlie was, for the perfect place to take the leap in Big Sur, see the big, white cross along the highway and come to their monastery instead. Many are saved.

All along this journey my sister held on to me and prayed with me — endless Rosaries. Finally they left me at San Jose airport for my trip home to all those waiting in even greater misery than I for not having said goodbye.

I believe that most parents know that the death of a child

would be the most excruciating thing one could ever experience. Who can measure such a thing? Not me. I don't think it would be better to watch a child die a slow death from a fatal disease, each moment praying for a healing that doesn't come. I don't think it would be better to try to turn the clock back to prevent a child from walking out the door at exactly six p.m., the only moment which would make it possible for him or her to be killed by a drunk driver at 6:10 p.m. Every "premature" death has its own particular variety of misery afterwards. Besides the sharp unendurable pain, there is depression, despair, disorientation, fatigue, guilt, intense emotional vulnerability in all other areas of personal relationship, and, in the case of suicide, an inability to make decisions (after all, if I didn't have the wisdom to help my child, how could any decision I ever make from now on have any validity?).

If you are trying to find comfort yourself after the suicide of your child or looking for ways to help a friend, I want to warn you that some advice is not helpful to some grieving mothers even if the intent of your words is sincere and loving.

For me, the worst suggestion was this: "Don't try to understand. It is all a mystery. Just give it all to God." This might sound good to a person whose general approach to life is through the idea of mystery, that is, one who doesn't like to analyze things, but loves to dwell in an ineffable wordless sense of God's Providence. It doesn't work with the type of Christian who takes his or her cue more from Job or Saint Catherine of Siena, that is, one who likes to talk things out with God until satisfied with an answer, however hard that answer might be. I would rather have been told, "Seek and you will find."

The second worst advice for me was "Just rest and let time heal it for you." A super-activist, I flourish, even when half-dead, on dynamic effort. I felt much better forcing myself out to work, at the seminary where I was teaching, surrounded by love and prayer, than brooding alone prostrate in bed.

To generalize from this experience, I now try to give advice that fits the known character of the person bereaved. I try to think how they might best go through the grieving process in modes that fit their individual personalities. For example, my poet daughter got some relief from writing a whole series of poems about her brother, to her brother, to God about her brother. My artistic daughter pored through all the family albums and made a collage of Charlie from babyhood to last photos. Tears streaming down her face, she managed to paste these images onto a large piece of cardboard. I brought this masterpiece to the funeral Masses and displayed it for the relatives and friends to see on the way to the pews. My husband, a writer, made excerpts from his son's suicide note which became a part of a six-page memorial booklet given to those closest to us. Several months later, he wrote a letter to his dead son, expressing his intense sorrow, yet his final acceptance.

I am a speaker. Some friends insisted I ought to cancel all the talks I had scheduled for the next year. I found, on the contrary, that it helped me to keep going. Even though choked with sobs, it was good to tell sympathetic audience about the special graces that came within a week of my son's death: how the clock stopped in our living room six hundred miles from where my son jumped; how, after the news, my husband heard his voice saying, "Don't worry, Dad, I'm okay"; how my sister heard him speak in her heart, saying that he was in a beautiful place, and finally how I heard Jesus speak in my heart telling me: "I let him jump because I could not stand to see his pain. He had his foretastes of eternity in the joys of his life. He was weaned by his pain from wanting life on earth. You will find him in my Heart." I end my talks now by asking all to join hands and pray for our family to be strengthened on our painful journey, and I get great solace from the hundreds of Mass cards that came with expressions of compassion.

A third and last type of advice I found hurtful involved friends who wanted us to accept their conclusions about what was wrong with our son. "Don't blame yourself, it is purely genetic," or "purely a matter of vitamin deficiency which rots the brain," or "a mental illness that leaves no room for any free will." I didn't mind people advancing these suggestions, but it was frustrating when they wanted to go on for hours insisting that theirs must be the explanation.

On the whole, however, most Christians have beautiful and helpful things to say. From priests what I wanted to hear and often got was "Your son is saved because ours is a God of mercy." Although vaguely aware that the Church no longer teaches that all suicides go to hell, because it is better understood in what kind of mental frenzy such decisions are made, there is still so much in the history and literature of the whole world about the evil of suicide that it takes many repeated proclamations about the mercy of God to reassure us. I now believe, that for many survivors of suicide, part of the good that God brings out of this evil is to force us to enter into the knowledge of his mercy. Many of us mouth words about this, but have never had to rely on his mercy as utterly as when ridden with anxiety about the fate of a beloved one whose death was not surrounded with signs of hope.

Even though it was very painful to see my son's friends, to try not to wonder why they are alive and not him, I found that, once in their presence, I loved it when they would reminisce about him and tell me how much his life enriched theirs. They have memories I don't have. His oldest friend, whom he knew from the age of five, started mimicking his voice and facial mannerisms and I was able to laugh and laugh through my tears.

Some friends just hugged me really hard and long and cried with me. One looked me straight in the eye and said: "I love you." I was surprised. How did he know how much I needed to hear that, since there was one precious son who would no longer say that until our reunion in eternity.

Here are some of the one-liners that helped my husband and me the most: A woman wrote in to Ann Landers' column saying that, after her child's death, she realized that, even if God had told her beforehand that she would only know her child for twenty years and then suffer so terribly over the death, she would prefer to have had that child to enjoy for a time. A nun wrote me: "Can you forgive yourself for not realizing that your son was weaker than you were?" A message on a card suggested that one carry on conversations with the one who died in the same light tone as if he or she were still in this life. A priest told me that I must die with my son in order to be resurrected with my son. Another said: "God didn't *call* Charlie home, but he *welcomed* him home."

A monk said that the Jesus who insists that "my burden is light" will let those die who cannot carry the burden. A dear friend slept in his bed and told me that in the night she heard my son interrupt her weeping: "Sing no sad songs for me." Another friend whispered: "Oh Ronda, think how much God trusts you to allow such a suffering to come to you, knowing that you would not rebel, that eventually you would believe that he can take care of your son and you, also." In a book about suicide, a mother says, "You will only feel better when you forgive the one who committed suicide and know that he or she is in a better place."

Does God allow such things to happen because only in this way can he bring us to the depths to cry out to him more urgently than ever before, to know him more urgently than ever before, to know him as our only Savior, and to find out how much we are loved by others who couldn't show so much love before when we were less needy? The pain of this death will never end . . . never? No, not never, for someday in heaven I will see my son running toward me. As Saint Thomas More said before his execution: "May we all meet again merrily in heaven, where all will be well, all will be very well."

A longer version of this tragic story can be found in my autobiography **En Route to Eternity**, *Miriam Press, 914/691-7271. I am touched when mothers say it helped them "Hold hands with God in the dark."*

Chapter Fourteen

Susan

I Told Him "No!"
Rape

Ronda: Many women have described the shock and misery of rape by a stranger. But rarely do we hear about rape by a friend, which carries its own special wounds.

Rape. It's a word I never used to give any thought to but is now one I have lived with for more than four years. It is a powerful word. Consequently, it is a word I use but rarely and very carefully. It is a word which describes an experience I have lived through but in no way describes it fully. How can one word hold so much pain?

It was a pleasant day in March, 1992. After morning Mass, I stopped by a friend and fellow music minister's apartment to drop off and discuss some music for the upcoming Easter Liturgies. I had known J for some months, having worked in the music ministry with him. He was not a Christian but worked as the choir's accompanist. I was young and naïve and a member of the choir. We had become friends. I was trying to show him Jesus, my precious friend. I wasn't sure of his goals, but he flattered me some and had been kind, although his promiscuous lifestyle was not hidden from me.

As we talked during the preceding few months, it became clear that he was entrenched in his immorality. I knew I was in over my head and had contacted a few friends who were older and more experienced and, I'd hoped, wiser. They agreed that I was probably not ready to minister to someone like J at that time, and one even urged me to totally end my relationship with him. I guess my friends' warnings were not strong enough. Led by my zeal, I was sure I could influence this man, sure I could help him recognize the void in his life and God's love for him. I was sure I could be an instrument for the Lord in his life. I was not a quitter, and besides, I saw so much good in J that I knew would be so much better with the benefit of God's mercy, love, forgiveness, and friendship. I knew he would be much more fulfilled serving God rather than himself.

So I stopped at his apartment that morning. After our business, we chatted a bit. Just as I was preparing to leave, I did something which "turned him on." I had no idea my action would have that effect on him. He let me know and tried to lure me into bed with him. I refused. I told him no, I would not, I could not. Well, he did anyway. He overpowered me (which was not too difficult given my small size) and had his way with me. I lay there in stunned silence. My mind was overcome with disbelief and shock. I had said no! I had not joked about it or been indirect. I had clearly refused his advances. How could this be happening? This is not happening! This *is* happening!

In this state of shock, I was overwhelmed with inertia. I had been coming down with a cold anyway, so I called in sick to work and went to sleep. J went off to his job. When I awoke, I was still in shock but no longer silent. I was hurting, angry, and afraid. I went home and telephoned every friend I could think of. I started with the women, and when none were available, moved on to the men. I knew I needed help and I had no idea how to get it. Finally, one of the men I knew was in. We arranged to meet in a nearby church after their noon Mass.

I arrived, tied in knots with tension. With a fair amount of coaxing, I told him what had happened. He comforted me without touching me and helped me get the help I needed. I was overwhelmed by my emotions and a great deal of fear, but driven by the conviction that I needed to get help — *now!*

I left the area a day or two later for a special hospital which could maintain my special diet for me while I got some help dealing with the fact that I had been raped. The day they did the pregnancy test was the hardest. I knew I would need to care for and love the baby, if there was one. It certainly was not the child's fault that he or she was conceived in this way. I nearly jumped out of my chair and kissed the doctor that afternoon when he told me that the test result was negative. I was not pregnant.

After a week in the hospital, I returned home and I told my parents. My parents were hurt that I had not told them immediately, and my dad was furious at J for what he had done. They never blamed me, thankfully, and were as supportive as I allowed them to be. As for me, I just needed to go home and heal.

My employer was most kind. I was placed on a special disability leave which allowed me to receive full pay and benefits while nothing was recorded on my employment record. My position was being eliminated in two months anyway, and they left it up to me as to whether I returned to the office or not. This gave me two months to do nothing but heal.

I took full advantage of the time I had. It was so obviously a gift to me. There were three things I did which most helped me heal. First, I continued to talk about what had happened. I quickly learned to be discreet, but I did talk about it. Second, I went to daily Mass. It just seemed to be the right thing to do and was vastly helpful to my healing process. Third, I got professional help. This was not something I could handle alone.

Going to Mass was healing in several ways. It daily forced me to face and overcome my fear of people. Seeing people helped me "return to normal." Since they had no idea of my pain, they treated me normally and invited me to treat them normally. This daily exercise was essential to my healing. It helped me regain my perspective and to slowly shift the focus from my own atrocities to the everyday activities, pains, and burdens of others. It also helped me to begin to overcome the fear which threatened to keep me locked within my apartment.

Daily Mass also helped me maintain my relationship with God in a time when I felt betrayed by him — why had he let this happen to me? My relationship with God had been strong for a long time and was now quite tenuous. I really struggled with trusting a good and loving God who seemed to have failed me when I had truly needed him. I repeatedly pushed this out of my mind, realizing that some initial healing was needed before I could handle this deep sense of betrayal. In time this came to the fore. The retreat I went to a few months later was pivotal in this portion of my healing.

The daily reception of the Body, Blood, Soul, and Divinity of my Lord and Savior Jesus Christ into my violated and seemingly defiled self was very healing. It told me that I was not truly defiled, that no matter how dirty I felt (and there were many days when I showered frequently trying to wash off that dirty feeling), I was *not* dirty. It told me that I was loved and accepted. It told me that I was worthy of life — which was an invaluable aid when the inevitable suicidal thoughts came.

I also saw a counselor during this time. I had wanted to see a woman, but things worked out such that I ended up seeing John. At first seeing a male therapist was very difficult. I was terrified, and he understood. He stayed at his desk on the other side of the room. I sat next to the door so I could escape if I felt the need to do so. His primary method was to help me think of myself in terms of parts — my angry part, my scared part, my betrayed part, my wounded part, and so on. I would be the "mom" for these parts. One by one we would address these parts of me and invite them to tell their stories. This method broke the huge mass of emotional distress down into manageable bits. This technique was absolutely invaluable for my healing. After letting the various parts of me tell their stories, John helped me take them to Jesus so my Savior could just hold them for a while or, when I was ready, make them whole. This was extremely difficult at first since I felt utterly abandoned by God, but I knew no one else who could help so, I was forced by necessity to begin to rebuild my trust in God.

I also went to some Twelve Step meetings. Although I validly belonged to the group, at this time these meetings simply provided me with some balance. Here I was reminded that others had pain, too. I was not the only person in the world who hurt and hurt deeply.

I tried to share my experience with some of my friends. Unfortunately, I found that many of them could not handle what I had been through and so my revelation brought those relationships to abrupt ends. This was not something I had expected, and these losses only added to my sufferings and my feelings of abandonment. Many of my friends had been men and most of them unfortunately handled my news very poorly. This was difficult for me but, I was buoyed up by others who repeatedly quoted Romans 8:28 to me. "We know that God makes all things work together for the good of those who love God. . . ." This was terribly hard to believe at first but, after hearing it cited by so very many people, I began to believe that it might be true. It became a beacon of light shining for me, giving me the hope and strength to persevere through the healing process.

During the therapy sessions, it became apparent that the feelings I was experiencing were not new to me. They strongly resonated with something deep inside me. It seemed obvious that a similar trauma had occurred at some time in my past. Neither John nor I thought that trying to remember would be helpful to my healing process so we did not try. Clearly, some of my life directions had been chosen in part because of the unconscious desire to protect deeply wounded areas. This meant that I needed to evaluate some decisions and possibly make some major changes in my life's direction. I spent a lot of time thinking and praying over these decisions. I realized that just because the motivation may have been imperfect, the decision may still have been the correct one to make. So, I tried to be cautious and thorough in my examinations of these areas.

For a short while after I returned from the hospital, it seemed that God's hand was over me in a special way. I was able to meet with J twice, in public places, of course. The first meeting was a gentle confrontation which culminated in his acceptance of what he had done. In the second meeting I was able to forgive him for his actions. Then God's shielding hand was removed and my rage came. I could see him no more — I was terrified of the rage — and I have not seen him again. Forgiving J was the right thing to do. I did not realize that it would help me heal by setting me free of resentment and other lingering emotional and spiritual baggage.

The final part of my healing began in late May, 1992. I went on a retreat. It was my first venturing forth and I was afraid. I went alone to a retreat called "A Pilgrimage of Trust." It was a gathering of approximately fifteen hundred young adults from all across North and Central America hosted by the Taizé monastic community from France. I certainly needed to grow in my trust both of God and of people, especially men. God had let me down, let this happen to me. He had not protected me.

Our relationship was on rocky ground; we were taking baby steps. Going to this retreat, stepping out in trust in this way was, for me, an attempt to start our relationship anew. I was giving God a second chance. I was risking everything again in the hopes that the Gospel really was true. The retreat was structured around communal prayer at morning, noon, and evening. I was part of the choir which led the chants. In between the prayer times were talks and small group discussions on various topics. Being in the choir was very scary at first. But as the days of the retreat wore on, it was as if I was being given back my voice. I could once again sing to the Lord.

Near the end of the retreat, a man came up to me and started telling me how my prayer during the retreat had inspired him. I was in a raw place emotionally and began to cry. I just wanted to be left alone; I did not want to trust. But he would not let me hide. He could tell something was hurting in me and wanted to help me heal. It seemed to me that he wanted to be Christ to me in that moment. I struggled mightily with trusting him. He was the first person at the retreat whom I had told of my pain and struggle. In order to end the encounter more quickly, I agreed to meet him the next day at the end of the retreat. Well, this second conversation lasted nearly six hours! We each finally went our separate ways home but kept up the conversation via frequent telephone calls and visits. That first conversation ultimately lasted over six months. In time, he proposed to me and, after slowly building trust and even love, we were married the next year. My healing had taken a major stride forward. During that year, there were several more strides made toward trusting God. It was difficult, but I was no longer alone on my journey.

We had a special, private agreement at our wedding. He freely agreed to wait to consummate our marriage until I was ready — no matter how long it took. I needed this assurance. I knew I was ready to be with this man for the rest of my life, but I also knew that this particular unitive step was going to require another leap of trust. This agreement gave me the freedom to really be ready for this intimate sharing. When the time came and I was ready, all went well. He was very gentle with me and with my scared and wounded parts, before acting. Thus he was finally invited into that private inner world where I was still healing. Once he had been admitted there, marital sharing could happen.

My healing process is not yet complete. Although I am no longer immobilized by fear, I still see a great deal of fear in myself as well as the warp it has caused in my personality. I trust that God will heal all in his own good time. My husband and I have been blessed with a child, and his presence in my life has brought more healing with it. And I trust that God will complete my healing in his own good time, one day at a time.

The author of this chapter wishes to remain anonymous.

Chapter Fifteen

Eileen Spotts

A Creature of God: Sexual Abuse

Ronda: Of all the many areas of pain reported by women to me during workshops, the one most devastating seems to be sexual abuse. What qualifies under this category can range from occasional illicit touching of a girl or teen, to frequent, regular violations imposed by several males within a family setting with a major betrayal of trust. A poet living in Sydney Australia, Helen Strano, included these lines in her books **Cycle of Madness** *and* **Road to Recovery** *[to order these books, write to her at P.O. Box 704, Petersham 2049, N.S.W., Australia].*

The cycle of life
becomes a cycle of madness
when dealing with the grief and loss
of childhood innocence . . .
loss of the child that couldn't be . . .
Always the question why?
Why me?
What was the matter with me
Why was I so hard to like . . .
what was wrong with me that they hurt me so. . . .
Was I so hard to like
I was but a girl

ugly and stupid they thought
But good enough to be used and abused by them
But not good enough to be loved and supported
Always the questions of why?"
— Helen Strano

Helen Strano's experience of sexual abuse was devastating. Through much counseling and prayer she now sees herself as a survivor. The young woman who wrote the piece "Overcoming Sexual Abuse" is coping with a less terrible experience. I asked Eileen to contribute her reflections because they provide such a hopeful way of being open to healing.

If today a small child came to me and said, "I didn't mean to go near that man, I really didn't," I would hold the little girl and touch her hair and soothe her. I would encourage her to cry. I would tell that beautiful little girl that she was a creature of God. He understood and it wasn't her fault. I would tell this little girl that it was good that she wanted to be touched and held. I would assure her that she would be loveable to her family and to God. I would tell her that sometimes grown-ups were confused and did things that hurt others because they themselves had been hurt.

As the little girl became a teenager, I would tell her that her interest in sex is natural. If she expressed an intense desire to be loved by a boy so much that she would let him take her clothes off, I would tell her that her neediness is a way of reaching out to fill that "hole in her soul." Unfortunately, her pleas for love will only lead to more emptiness. If she confessed that she entertained sexual fantasies from romance novels and magazines and that she needed to release the sexual tension through frequent masturbation, I would help her to see that this shame-filled habit is also rooted in her woundedness. By objectifying men for pleasure, her conscience would be inundated by lust.

I would tell this teenage girl that although everyone around her was exploring one another sexually, that she was different. I would assure her that she was a unique creature of God and that he had a plan for her life. His plan was her full redemption — her soul, her body, and her mind. He also redeemed her sexuality.

I would show her how he created her to be feminine and how he loved her and continually asks her to trust him. I would show this teenage girl that she could be strong, that she could face the temptations because he would give her the grace to stay a virgin so that she could be a greater gift to her husband.

As the little girl would become a woman, I would listen to her remorse if she talked about the emptiness that premarital sexuality offered her. I would listen to her anguish that her present boyfriend would not commit to her. I would ask her to tell me how angry she is. I would listen to her bitterness, her distaste for men, her rage toward men and those who were in authority over her. I would listen to her quest for freedom and her desire to gain power in her life, which might be expressed by seeking guidance from radical feminists who seemed to have it all. I would hear her desire to be free and rid of all the pain.

I would take her hand in mine, look her square in the eye, and tell her that God has a better plan. His mercy would offer her healing if only she could muster the strength to reach out and trust him. I would recognize that she has difficulty in trusting his masculinity or his fatherhood because of her negative experiences.

I would tell her that Mary would guide her if she could let her in her heart. Mary was also woman who was betrayed by the world. She persevered in hope for a better life. She trusted in God and he led her through the suffering to eternal happiness. In God's mercy, he gave us his mother as his great and final gift. I would encourage her to examine the anguish he was in when he gave of his heart so freely.

He had been betrayed, deserted by those closest to him, humiliated, beaten, mocked, and stripped. He was nailed to the cross and lifted for all to see with only loin cloth, if that, to cover him. After giving us so much love, the Lord died with practically no clothes on his body. This was a form of sexual abuse, too. He took on our sins so that we could be free to have a life — a life free of the bondage of empty lies and sinful behavior. The only way to receive this life of greater beauty is to reach out to him, the shepherd, and allow him to restore our identity. I would tell this woman that she was made in God's image, in his image she was created (Gn 1:26). I would tell her that God saw her as good. I would tell her that if she had sinned, he knew how sorry she was for hurting others with her misguided sexuality. I would tell her that now it was time to forgive herself and to move forward with her life. She could not erase the past but she could refuse to let it haunt her and destroy her self-image. She is now a new creature in Christ and he will never abandon her. Even if she felt rejected by a lover or her parents, God saw her as very, very good. He even offers himself to her in a special way through the sacraments.

He also offers her a shelter under the mantle of his mother's love. I would tell her that Mary wants to love her so deeply and she wants to show her ways of authentic God-given femininity. God gave Mary to us so that we can be intimate with him as part of the family. She was part of Christ, and would be forever in his loving arms if only she would accept him as her love.

She need not feel ugly or unworthy any more. I would tell her that now was the time to take her place in the circle of life. No fear could stand in the way of God's love for her. She must accept his healing and allow him to transform her heart. I would tell her that her life would be very full of adventure and of life-giving love.

Eileen Spotts holds master's degrees in Psychology and Theology from Franciscan University of Steubenville. She is a Catholic business woman.

Chapter Sixteen

Lynn Cordano

Even in Darkness, the Light of Christ Heals: Sexually Abused Mother of Abused Children

Ronda: I met Lynn as a woman I would enjoy praying with. As her story unfolded, I knew it would not be unique and that it belonged in this book.

The knife. I remember the knife. There was a terrible ruckus. My father was screaming obscenities as he dragged me from my bed to the kitchen, without my feet ever touching the floor. I was three. My father yanked open the kitchen drawer so hard that all the silverware clanked to the back, then to the front. Still screaming at me with a fury beyond anything I had ever seen in my Dad, he grabbed the biggest butcher knife we had and shoved me over to the kitchen table.

My father shrieked, "Don't you know that it's a mortal sin to masturbate? You'll go to HELL for this!" Then, slamming my tiny little hands down on the table, he yelled amidst continued obscenities, "If I ever catch you again, I will cut your fingers right off!" In a cutting motion he moved the blade back and forth over those little fingers, just close enough to scare the life out of me.

This first incident was so permanently etched upon the pages of my mind that the next forty or so years of my life were, to a great extent, a reflection of it. Perhaps it is so horrible even to read about that you think I may have made it up. I sometimes thought that too, but once I started to tell my sister about it and she yelled "Stop, I don't want to hear anymore!" Tears ran down her face as she clasped her hands tightly over her ears. She remembered the knife, too!

As is the case with many children who were sexually abused, I did not remember the abuse at all for a long time. My memory was selective. I remembered only that my father told me I had committed a mortal sin. And the knife! What a dreadful fear I have of knives. Still today, at the very thought or sight of a knife, I feel the blade drawn across my lips. You will only find serrated knives in my kitchen. They do not seem as deadly.

I was too little to know that masturbating at age three could not be a mortal sin, nor did I know until many years later that I had not been masturbating at all. My father's words were a cover for having been caught in the act of incest; his rage, a result of his own fear.

Into this darkness came the light of Jesus. He came to me in Church, when I was between three and four. Like all good Catholics, my parents would faithfully drag themselves to confession once a month. Their devotion was limited, but fear made up for whatever might have been lacking in faith.

My older sister and I were supposed to wait quietly in a pew while our parents stood in the long confessional line. Bored, my sister and I used to pass the time writing on the little church envelopes with those stubby pencils that always fit neatly into the holes provided in the compartment on the backs of each pew. We also delighted in walking along the kneelers like tightrope walkers in a circus.

It was during one such Saturday that Christ bathed me in grace. Without knowing why, I ceased my activities and sat down quietly in a pew. My sister continued to play. I felt an inexplicable presence surrounding me. I don't mean from a distance; I was breathing this presence. I fixed my gaze on the large crucifix above the altar. I saw no vision, I heard no audible voice, but I breathed love!

In the silence of my heart I promised never to commit a mortal sin, and wrapped in His loving embrace, a long drawn out *yes* flowed from my lips. From that moment on I began dressing up like a nun to play school or church with all the others kids in the neighborhood. Mom and Dad thought it was cute, but to me it was real. The "yes" that came from my lips was a response to Christ, who, I somehow understood, had asked me to be his bride.

The incest continued until I was about ten. Often, my mother was an observer and sometimes a reluctant participant. I was also made to visit a doctor and his wife next door on a regular basis, for the same purposes. There was a special room for me there.

My First Communion, at age seven, gave me the refuge I needed to see me through these years of horror. When the priest put the Host on my tongue for the first time, I knew I was with the bridegroom of my soul, and I was in heaven, even if for a short time. I reveled in the promise of being his bride.

In many ways I led two lives. One was the normal, growing, young person that my parents and society insisted upon. The other was my hidden life in Christ. He was my hiding place in the cleft of the rocks. I felt I possessed a secret to which no one else was privy.

As I got older, these experiences were hidden somewhere in my memory. I was left with a vague feeling of being alone, and afraid, unworthy, and guilty. I remember swinging for hours in our backyard, with my eyes lost in the clouds, hoping upon hope that God would take me up there with him.

Prayer became my hiding place, even when I was very

young. I remember being "caught" praying on several occasions, feeling a sense of guilt, as if I had been doing something wrong I began reading children's lives of the saints, feeling drawn in particular to those whose suffering was extreme.

After my senior year in high school, I entered an order of sisters. During the postulancy and novitiate I flourished, becoming more truly myself than I had ever been allowed to be in my life. I was utterly in love and inexplicably happy.

The problems began when we were sent out of the motherhouse with its beauty, peace, silence, and unhurried pace to pursue further education and to practice-teach in a crowded classroom with fifty-two first graders. Even though I was an immediate success as a teacher, my growing inner turbulence was unmistakable. I felt unworthy and restless outside the contemplative environment of the motherhouse.

In desperation when no one seemed able to help me, I asked for a leave and dispensation from my vows. It broke my heart to sign the final papers.

Not knowing quite what to do, I decided to spend a few weeks with my sister and her family. Taking a job teaching second grade worked out well. I began dating several young men. The one I would eventually decide to marry seemed like a good person. He was a good Catholic, four years older than me. I was never attracted to this man on any level. But I did appreciate his intelligence and his seriousness about his profession as an investigator for the Federal Food and Drug Administration.

The passivity with which I agreed to marry a man I didn't love later seemed to me a symptom of having been sexually abused as a child. Our engagement was stormy — my fiancé seemed utterly obsessed by fear. He seemed close to a breakdown from fears that had no definition. When I talked of breaking the engagement, he agreed to seek help from a counselor. This advisor told me that my intended had some rather serious problems, but that he was very much in love with me. I felt that even though I didn't love him, he needed me and that I could make him happy.

On my wedding day I begged God to forgive me for leaving my true bridegroom to get married.

At first, everything went well. I had two lovely girls within two years and later a precious son. My older daughter loved to mother her little sister, who began to develop severe health problems. After many perplexing, heartbreaking emergencies I had to face the fact that my second daughter was disabled with either rheumatoid arthritis or lupus. I felt certain that God was punishing me for my childhood sins of masturbating and for having left the convent.

My husband reacted by retreating more into himself.

Night after night I knelt by my daughter's crib, pleading with God to take her illness away and give it to me. I deserved to suffer, not her. Although these diseases are incurable, after my fervent prayers, my daughter was diagnosed as totally healed. God had taken me at my word. I was diagnosed with lupus. But my daughter was slow in her development. Later I realized this was because of things done to her by her father. Her behavior was strange — sometimes she seemed completely normal and happy, at others miserable.

By the time my little ones were six, seven, and eight, my marriage had deteriorated. My husband thought all was well. True, he was a good provider. After ten years of marriage we embarked on an intense program of marriage counseling. I felt that I was a mother figure to my husband. Our sex life was by then nonexistent. It seemed clear to me that my husband didn't like the kids. He might have loved them, but he didn't like them. When they tried to get close to him, he would push them away.

The stress manifested itself for me in twenty-six ulcers to top off the lupus. I went down to eighty-three pounds. I seemed to be dying. I was anointed. During this crisis I made a promise to myself that if I ever made it through the surgery that was performed to prevent my stomach from bursting, I would take my kids and leave.

When I recovered, I went to my sister's house until I could

get a teaching position and get my own place. I started divorce proceedings.

During the next few months my husband's behavior became erratic and often violent. On one occasion I stopped at the house with my three kids to pick up the mail. He was at work and I had the key. Upon entering the kitchen, the kids and I were appalled to find large hate notes scrawled on paper with black pen taped all over the kitchen walls! I was seized with fear. I got the kids out of there as fast as I could. Later, with great caution, I went back and took pictures of each note, forty or fifty in all.

When my attorney saw these notes, we decided it was unsafe for my husband to be alone with the children. I requested of the court that I be allowed to be present when my husband would see them the first six months after the divorce. Because of this request, the entire family was directed to appear for a consultation in reconciliation court. The children and I went one day, my husband on another.

The counselor came out after the interviews with tears in his eyes. "I don't know how a man with three such precious children could not love them" was his poignant comment.

One week later both my husband and I received a response from the court. The court decided that my husband not be allowed to see his three children ever again or even talk to them! Within hours after receiving this news, my husband was in the emergency room at the hospital with severe pain. It looked like a gall bladder attack. In the process of surgery, they found nothing to explain the pain, but they damaged his pancreas. It seemed he lost all desire to live. On the sixth day after the surgery, he was clinically dead for a period of ten minutes. While the doctors and nurses worked on him, I knelt only feet away, holding the Eucharist close to my heart; the Host which he was now unable to receive.

In those moments between life and death, it was given to me as a grace to have an interior vision of the meaning of Isaiah 54, verses four through ten:

147

"Fear not, for you will not be ashamed;
　be not confounded, for you will not be put to
　　shame;
for you will forget the shame of your youth,
　and the reproach of your widowhood you will
　remember no more.
For your Maker is your husband;
　the LORD of hosts is his name:
and the Holy One of Israel is your Redeemer,
　the God of the whole earth he is called.
For the LORD has called you
　like a wife forsaken and grieved in spirit,
like a wife of youth when she is cast off,
　says your God.
For a brief moment I forsook you,
　but with great compassion I will gather you.
In overflowing wrath for a moment
　I hid my face from you,
but with everlasting love I will have compassion
　on you,
　says the LORD, your Redeemer.

My husband was revived. For twenty-five days he lived on a respirator, bleeding to death; his pancreas consumed all the organs in his body. He died.

Life changed drastically for our little family. Though we were all sad, there was an unmistakable peace. The next year was the happiest we ever experienced. Although I often wondered why the court had come to such a drastic decision and if it had caused my husband's death, I tried not to think about it, wanting to leave all that behind.

Over the next several years my children began to change. One was disruptive, another rebellious. One got involved with pot and drinking.

In desperation I decided to try to find out more about that judgment concerning their father. A long search led to the psychologist who had been responsible for the decision. When I called him on the phone, I was stunned to find that he remembered all about us. He said it was because he had never encountered a sadder case!

At the time of the interview, the law prevented him from telling me the truth. My husband had molested all three of my children, most likely from the time they were tiny babies!

My heart sank. I hung up the phone and sobbed bitterly. That was what had been so wrong! That was why my kids were sick all the time. How could I have been so blind, so stupid? How could I have let that happen to my precious children? Oh God, no!

I arranged to have my girls taken into a mental health facility. During the month they were there, one of them would cry and pound her fists on the table, wailing over and over again "Why did he have to do that to me?" The older girl didn't remember having been abused. But she began to act it out by getting into topless dancing. By contrast, the younger one became involved in a wonderful teen program at our church. Miracles of grace happened for her in this outreach ministry.

My son, who had not seemed to need therapy, benefited greatly from the help of a fine young man in the Big Brother program who could substitute somewhat for his missing father. Even so, he became involved with drugs in high school, frequently missing school.

In June, 1992, as part of a master's program in Pastoral Theology/Spirituality, I made a thirty-six-day silent directed retreat as part of the Ignatian exercises.

The sister who was my director led me into deep healing prayer for my childhood. When the memories I have only outlined at the beginning surfaced, I became violently ill, and had to be treated in the emergency room twice. I kept trying to convince myself that I was making it all up. As I doubled over in pain and vomited, my director would remind me that the body doesn't lie. Some of the memories were so horrible that I would crouch in the corner of my bed at night and beg: "Please God, no more, not tonight, I am so afraid!" But he was relentless, and in pain, I would remember again.

I came to understand that my abuse didn't end with my father and mother, or with the neighbor. It continued on in my husband, who for all practical purposes *was* my father. Often during this time I would say my husband's name when I meant my father, or the other way around. My pain, and that of my children seemed more than I could bear.

I had been abused so severely over such a long period of time that I truly believed I had gotten exactly what I deserved. I believed I was a terrible person, totally undeserving of love. I certainly didn't deserve to be a nun, nor to be happy, or to have healthy kids, or to be healthy myself. I deserved my husband! With all the pain of reliving these experiences, came a flood of anger: properly directed anger. "My God! It wasn't me, I'm not awful, You don't hate me!" It was probably the healthiest emotion I had ever experienced.

I found myself a long walking stick. For hours at a time, I would walk the paths of that beautiful mountain where I was on retreat, and scream and cry and beat the dickens out of the shrubs beside the path.

There was one more question. What about God? Why had he let all this happen? So much pain; so much sorrow? I had always known he had "chosen" me, but did he love me? Did he really love me? My director responded one day: "Lynn, he died on the cross for you; of course he loves you." In anger I snapped back: "Anybody can do something for three hours; I've been suffering for forty-five years!"

The day before the retreat was over, I asked the priest if I could make a general confession. I felt so dirty; so ashamed to look at God. Would he ever see me as clean? Everyone else said I was okay, but I wanted to hear it from God. Even though the priest reassured me that there had been no sin in my victimization, my gut told me it wasn't over. Finally he agreed to hear my confession. When he laid his hands on my head and prayed,

God unleashed such a miracle of healing grace that I left the retreat a completely different person.

I know that putting this great grace in words will make it sound trite, but words are all I have.

I never understood until the moment of this grace that Jesus Christ died for me! He suffered terrible agonies because I suffered terrible agonies! He allowed himself to be stripped of his clothing and humiliated and abused and spit upon because I had been abused and humiliated! He allowed himself to be bloodied with thorns and nails because I too had shed my blood!

He allowed himself to know utter abandonment because I had been so abandoned by my father and mother! I understood for the first time, that there is not one thing I have ever suffered, or will ever suffer, that he himself has not suffered first.

He filled me with hope! When I was young, I seemed to know this; I had simply forgotten it as I grew older.

That moment of grace has so filled me with hope, that I believe, even in the darkness, that my children too, will come to know his love. I see him suffering in them, in their confusion and doubt, their fear and anger, even in their self-destructive behavior.

I see him suffering in all his little ones. We are his little ones, his body, the Church.

But his death, our deaths, are not the end, but the beginning. Because he rose from the dead, so too will we. *That* is the Paschal Mystery! *That* is what happens every time we celebrate Eucharist! In him is our *hope*, our *joy*, our *peace*!

We can say with Paul to Timothy: If we have died with him, we will also live with him; if we endure, we will also reign with him (2 Tim 2:11-12).

Lynn Cordano is a widow and mother, a school teacher with a master's degree in Pastoral Theology/Spirituality. She is a lay contemplative living under vows.

Chapter Seventeen

Paulette Bernadette

Meeting Christ in Multiple Sufferings: Physical, Emotional, and Spiritual Pain

Ronda: Perhaps you are reading these chapters and thinking — yes, these women found out how to hold hands with God in darkness, but none of them have been as afflicted as I am. So I am sure this witness will change your mind. May it bring to you as it did to me cleansing tears of empathy and awe."Nothing is impossible with God."

My name is Paulette, and I'm an alcoholic-addict. I am also schizophrenic and a chronic depressive. I am neurologically impaired in all four limbs and suffer constant pain. I am a child of God and I have a right to be here. Only my Father in Heaven has the right to take me to him when he pleases. I am valuable as a person. I unite my sufferings, joys, and daily life to Jesus' Holy Sacrifice on the Altar, on his Holy Cross, for the salvation of souls and in reparation for sin. I am living the spiritual works of mercy. Do not kill me please, as you will not be doing me a favor. I need to grow in God and my suffering enables me to do that. I love you and I lay my life down for you in my suffering. Jesus did that for you and for me. Please let me continue loving you. It is what he asks of all of us, that we, "Love one another even as I have loved you." (Jn 13:34)

I was born February 22, 1942, in California in a charity ward of a county hospital. My natural mother made up my last name. My natural father had already abandoned us for he was married to someone else. To this day I know almost nothing about him except his name and that he played the piano and organ at the nightclub where my mother sang for a living. I learned later that he was a "real alcoholic," and that when she told him she was pregnant with me while they were driving down a country road, he said, since he was married already, "If I can't have you, no one else will." He then ran the car into a tree attempting to kill all of us. No one was hurt seriously, but I had convulsions at birth and almost died.

My earliest memory was of standing up in a crib and screaming to an empty, strange house because I had dropped my bottle between the slats onto the floor. No one came for a long time.

I lived with my natural mother until age five or so, when she and one of her boyfriends, who had sexually molested me shortly before, dumped me at a Catholic orphanage for about two years. I withdrew. I did not speak, nor play with the other children. I got all "F's" in kindergarten and first grade. I wet the bed almost daily, and the dormitory Sister would make me sit on a stool at the foot of the bed with the wet sheet over my head until she thought it was long enough. Then I had to carry the sheets across the school yard in front of all the children to the laundry Sister. The laundry Sister was kind and gave me a cup of grape juice to drink. In later years, when I had anxiety, I'd get the taste of grape juice in my mouth and be comforted. When I started drinking, my favorite was red port wine — fermented dark grape juice.

I fell while in this orphanage and broke my tailbone. They did nothing about it. I woke up with gum in my hair, because I

153

went to sleep with it in my mouth, and the dormitory Sister shaved half my hair. My hair was the only thing I had that I was proud of. I had short curly hair "like Shirley Temple," others said.

The only good things I remember at the orphanage were the Mass every day; the prayers and devotions, songs and processions in honor of Our Lady; and the little statue of the Infant of Prague left under my pillow in place of a tooth I'd lost the night before. I remember the glazed donuts and hot chocolate we had every Wednesday, too. But my only real consolations were Jesus and Mary. They comforted me in my abandonment.

When I was seven and one-half, my natural mother took me out of the orphanage (after no contact since she dropped me off at age five) and we went to live with my aunt for a short time. While there, one of my cousins and I played "nuns" in the backyard, wearing old curtains for veils and our mothers' high heels, with our hands folded, and pious looks on our faces. We were missionaries going to save the "pagan babies" of some distant land like China.

One afternoon the couple who were to be my adopted parents came and took me. There were no good-byes, no indication of what was truly happening. Three days later I asked my adopted mother (whom I shall refer to from now on as "Mother"), "When am I going to see my Mommy?"

She replied, "Didn't they tell you?"

"Tell me what?"

"You're never going to see your Mommy again."

I screamed and cried for three days and nights.

My life with my adopted parents was stressful to say the least. At age seven and one-half I had my first alcoholic drink. My grandpa, my adopted father's father who lived with us, gave me a "hot toddy" for a cold which was hot lemon juice, honey, and a double shot of Old Crow whiskey. I loved how it made me feel. I got many colds after that!

At eight I made my First Holy Communion. This was the most important event ever in my whole life that I remember.

(Of course, Baptism was too, but I don't remember that, having been baptized at age one and one-half). I fell in love with Jesus. I was in Catholic school now and the nuns taught me, that Jesus is God, that he loved me so much he died for me, and that he was really truly present in Holy Communion. We had to prepare with prayer for three days, and the afternoon before with the sacrament of Penance to purify our souls so they'd be clean for Jesus to come there as our guest. I was so happy. For the first time I truly knew love from love himself.

I wanted to become a nun — to be the "Bride of Christ" like I was told my natural mother had become when she gave me up for adoption. It wasn't until I was eleven that I learned the real reason for my adoption: my natural mother was pregnant with my little sister. My natural mother had not gone to any convent. I was jealous and felt doubly abandoned.

Somewhere before age eleven, I was beaten with a braided leather dog leash by my adopted mother for having been caught in a lie. I learned to lie better after that.

When I was eleven years old, my pediatrician prescribed daily wine and codeine for cramps after I began having severely painful periods. I started going to Mass a lot during the week and on Saturdays. There was no love at home. My dad was always at work, drunk, or asleep. My mother and father fought a lot about money, and about other women my mother thought my father had known before they adopted me. I learned my mother had wanted a boy, but couldn't get him, and I was second choice. Daddy wanted me because I looked like his mother. Mother accused him of being my real father. The only love I got was from Jesus and the dogs we had in the backyard.

At thirteen I made my confirmation and wanted to become a soldier in Christ's army of the Church Militant in the Mystical Body of Christ. I fell in love with Saint Sebastian, an early Roman martyr, and I fell in love with Saint Thérèse of Lisieux and the Carmelites after reading her autobiography. I wanted to become a Carmelite, too, one day.

But at home things were horrible. Mother began having rages — screaming so loud it hurt my ears. I could do nothing right. I was never good enough; I was in torment and extreme fear of the Hitler she was becoming. She frequently threw things, stamped her feet, and slapped me across the face in front of others. My dad did nothing. At first I thought him stoic. Then I called him "yellow," a "Milquetoast," and a coward. He simply drank himself to sleep every night so as not to deal with mother.

At fourteen, I attempted suicide for the first of many times in my life. It was a cry for help and I made sure my best friend at school saw me. She told Sister Superior, who forced my parents to send me to a psychiatrist. Unfortunately he was not helpful and was also too expensive for my parents. I quit seeing him after three months. The focus in my family now became "What are we going to do with Paulette?"

Anger, rebellion, and confusion ruled my inner life now. I even blamed God and began doubting his existence. He seemed far from me — even gone. At seventeen, I got drunk for the first time while watching "Rebel Without a Cause," identifying with James Dean. It felt great. I felt powerful for the first time.

At eighteen I had my first cigarette — again, out of rebellion and a false sense of power.

In college at nineteen I was given Librium to calm my frayed nerves. I was working nights and going to school days. I was anorexic and bulimic; I took No-Doz and lived on alcohol, cigarettes, caffeine, and candy bars. I weighed ninety-eight pounds. In my junior year after another suicide attempt, I was committed to a state mental hospital with severe catatonic schizophrenia and depression. I was twenty-two years old. I went in and out of mental hospitals about five times a year until I was thirty-eight. I received more than twenty electric shock treatments, half of which I felt and remember vividly. My memory of what happened in my life immediately before and after the shock treatments has disappeared forever. I had to relearn almost everything. In spite of it all, I got my bachelor's degree, although I was never able to hold a job after that for any length of time as I would "break down" emotionally and mentally. I was stoned on tranquilizers all the time.

At thirty-three I developed multiple drug and food allergies and so I had to stop drinking and drugging. It was awful! I had eczema all over my body and I felt like Job. I hated God for doing this to me, though I didn't give up praying altogether. I kept asking him to help me. I begged and pleaded, but felt totally abandoned. I saw Billy Graham preach and took Jesus as my Lord and Savior. I asked the Holy Spirit to come and take over my soul. Nothing appeared to be happening except the continuation of my intense suffering.

During this time, mother threatened to kill Daddy and me in our sleep by turning on the gas or burning down the house or poisoning our food. It was truly a crazy house. I was living in fear of her, God, and the world. I was so sick, yet began to study the Bible — especially prophecy.

At thirty-five I was severely catatonic and almost died. My psychiatrist said, "You're going to die if you don't move away from home." I knew what he said was true. I went to a board-and-care home, but they told me to leave because they couldn't handle my food allergies. I was now on a reduced dose of Valium — the only tranquilizer I could take now, since my drug tolerance had severely dropped.

One of my cousins found an apartment for me and helped me move. Since I continued to go in and out of hospitals, my psychiatrist told me, "You must go either to a locked mental facility or to a day-treatment center and begin working yourself." I knew if I went to a locked facility, I wouldn't get the special laundry soap or body soap I needed because of my allergies; nor would I get the special food I needed. I would suffer more there. So I chose instead to got to the day-treatment center — for the next two and one-half years. While I was there, my

157

dad died of lung cancer and cirrhosis of the liver. Two months later, my mother died of blood clots in both lungs while she was in a mental ward.

For the first time in my life I felt free! I was thirty-eight years old. I inherited a house and a lot of bills so I had to sell the house to pay the bills. I had enough money to go to Europe with a religious group tour. We went to the Holy Land, Rome, and Lourdes. When I was immersed in the waters at Lourdes I had a spiritual experience. I asked Our Lady to cure my allergies. She did cure most of my food allergies, but not my drug allergies. I couldn't figure out why till a year and a half later when I came into a Twelve-Step Program and got clean and sober at age forty-one.

Before I went to Europe, I had begun a relationship with a man who was an alcoholic, and this continued for more than five years. I slept with many other men, too. Thank God, I didn't get AIDS.

Six months after the European trip I found out I could eat normally again, and thought: "Wine is made from grapes; grapes are a food; maybe I can drink again." I started drinking as well as taking the Valium. At this time I noticed that my boyfriend drank like my dad, who had just died of an alcohol-related disease. It scared me. I began talking about it in the small therapy groups at the day-treatment center I was still going to, and they suggested I go to an Al-Anon meeting which met on the grounds once a week.

I coerced my boyfriend to go with me to AA. He had the problem — not me, I thought. But going to Al-Anon broke down my denial. I was not only a co-dependent, but an alcoholic-addict as well! I was sure I could "do it myself" by trying to quit alcohol and Valium without meetings, but it didn't work. Finally, I broke down and cried in an Al-Anon meeting. I declared I was an alcoholic-addict for the first time out loud, and asked for help. They suggested going into the treatment center for thirty days, which I did. We got intensive AA teaching while there, and my withdrawals were pretty bad, but I hung in. They stressed going to meetings, "working" the steps and getting a sponsor right away.

Two days after I left the treatment center I went to an AA meeting because I was scared. When I told them that I was scared, they said "That's all right, just keep coming back. It gets better." So I did. I couldn't relate to my sponsor and didn't share in meetings, so after thirty more days I had a Valium slip (I had kept a stash for an "emergency"). Immediately, my drug hunger came back and I got frightened and called my sponsor. She told me to flush the rest of the pills and get to a meeting. I was so afraid. I didn't get to the meeting for twenty-four hours, though I did flush the rest of the Valium along with some Demerol I'd kept. I thought they'd tell me to leave AA because I'd failed, but they didn't. They told me instead, "Keep coming back" and "Let us love you until you can love yourself." I was praying a little every day now, since AA encouraged it, and I was getting monthly counseling from a Catholic priest.

At this time I was sleeping with my boyfriend on a regular basis, having occasional one-night stands with other guys whenever my regular boyfriend and I would break up, smoking heavily, using foul language on a regular basis, dressing immodestly, telling myself I was mostly sinless — all the while, going to Mass and Communion every Sunday, but rarely going to confession.

Meanwhile I was seriously studying the steps in the Step Study meetings and the "Big Book" which describes AA's program for living without alcohol. I was facing my history of physical and emotional abuse and abandonment in Adult Children of Alcoholics meetings, as well as dealing with co-dependent issues in Al-Anon. In spite of my sinful lifestyle, the Lord was firmly but gently bringing me toward him.

I had always been afraid of God the Father because of my parents' abuse and abandonment of me, and my misunderstanding of him in the Old Testament. I loved Jesus, but was afraid of him, too. I had no concept of the Holy Spirit at this time, although he was performing mightily in me with his most loving and generous graces.

I kept asking God to help me change and grow, and he began answering my prayers. My boyfriend and I were both smokers. He decided *we* were going to go to a new program, Nicotine Anonymous, and *we* were going to quit *together*. Ha! I wasn't too sure I wanted to quit. I thought I'd get fat and/or have a mental breakdown, but I went with him. They say going to meetings spoils your addiction — it breaks down your denial, and it's true. I tried to quit with him, but couldn't do it. I got on my case about it, beating myself up emotionally because "I should be able to do this — I have been clean and sober for more than three years.!"

At this time I began to see, because of the readings in the Step Study and Big Book meetings, that I was using my boyfriend as a drug — using sex as a drug — and letting him use me as a drug — so I could feel accepted. I began to see how my use of foul language was not right and tried to clean up my mouth. I saw the way my boyfriend treated me — he was good to me in many ways and was generous too, but he was also verbally abusive to me, as I was also to him. When things didn't go well — even when they did — there was verbal abuse. I saw my adopted parents in myself and my boyfriend, as if we were clones of them. It was incredible. For almost a year I saw all of this by stepping mentally outside of myself and observing our relationship. I read a book on women who "love too much" and saw myself (I didn't want to break up with him). I was groaning inside, knowing I had to change, yet terrified to do so.

Christmas came and my boyfriend had stopped smoking for one month but I still couldn't quit. He got on my case all the time about it. It was pouring rain and freezing cold that night, and he wouldn't let me smoke in his apartment. We had just opened all our presents and I went outside to smoke with coat, hat, and mittens on, with the tops of the fingers cut off so I could hold the cigarette. I was freezing. He even had an empty coffee can there, for my butts, so as not to dirty his garden. I began thinking of the past year and my observations. "Was this relationship worth the trouble to smoke in the cold and rain, together with everything else?" "No," I answered myself. I went inside and started crying as I looked at him and said, "I can't do this anymore. I can't continue to sleep with you and live with myself. Either you marry me or I have to stop seeing you."

Of course, he didn't have the slightest idea as to what was going on, but restated his usual position that he couldn't marry me because I wasn't good enough for him. In reality, it was his fear of responsibility, not me. I left him that Christmas Day. That was the hardest thing I've ever done in my life. I truly was addicted to him and now I had to go through the withdrawals. I was devastated with an empty hole inside me, so I went to a meeting and cried in front of everyone. I received a lot of love from all the people there. They gave me courage, but I still didn't have God. I prayed yet God seemed so far away. I wanted to die, I hurt so bad, yet I was so afraid of change. I began thinking about suicide, so I signed myself into a psych unit where I also went through alcohol and drug treatment. While there, I regressed into catatonia, but it wasn't the same. I had changed in spite of myself. I couldn't use mental illness to escape reality anymore. Reality was hitting me in the face full force.

And then God came into my life as he had never been before. Before my eyes, my whole life flashed, and I *saw*. For the first time I *saw* how God was there for me, with me, and through other people helping me throughout my life, *every step of the way*. He had never left me. *I had left him!* I knew what I had to do, only now I knew I didn't have to do it alone. I acknowledged that only a power greater than myself could restore me to sanity and turned my life and will over to the care of God. I began to trust God because I began to know his love for me. I sought him through AA and I found him through the fellowship as they loved and accepted me unconditionally. I began to see God, to love him again, and not be so fearful of change.

I was still going to ACA and began to love myself and nurture myself. I saw I could be the parents I never had. I mourned for the little child inside me who was love-starved. Although I had abandoned myself before, I now saw that I was an adult and that I could take care of myself. I saw that I had a loving Father who was taking care of me all along, but I needed to get closer to him.

I needed to get clean again. I went to confession — a general confession. I quit all immorality, profanity, and smoking. I began eating normally instead of starving or binging. I spent more time with God in prayer and spiritual reading. I spoke about my spiritual conversion in meetings.

I chose to live a celibate and chaste life and so I prayed to Our Lady for purity; she continues to help me live a chaste life. I realized the Church was indeed our mother, and that she is truly wise in all she teaches. I saw that I had to obey God's commandments and I couldn't be a "Cafeteria Catholic" like so many of my friends. I fell in love with God the Father, Jesus, and the Holy Roman Catholic Church. I began reading about my Faith again "seeing" clearly for the first time what the good Sisters tried to teach me in twelve wonderful years of Catholic school. I loved the nuns, I loved Catholic school, and again fell in love with my Church, my Faith, and my God.

I went to a charismatic prayer group at my church where I was "slain in the spirit," received the gift of tongues and the gift of prophecy. I joined the choir and became active in my parish.

For a year I lived as I was supposed to according to God's will, not mine. Then my aunt, who was Formation Directress of the Third Order of Carmelites, noticed the change and realized it was a true conversion. She invited me to become a Third Order Carmelite! I was so surprised! So happy! So thankful to God who was blessing me so abundantly! All my life I had wanted to be a nun and, since seventh grade, a Carmelite! I couldn't join a convent because I was too ill, but here God was, inviting me to be his bride in the world — a lay Carmelite!

I cried, and said "Yes!" I was a postulant for one and one-half years and a novice for two years, continually growing spiritually under the wise guidance of my aunt and our dear spiritual director. I prayed the Rosary almost daily, the Little Office of Our Lady of Mount Carmel, and later the regular Liturgy of the Hours. I went to confession every first Saturday, returning to devotions and novenas I used to pray in grammar school. I read the lives of the saints again. I went to Mass and Communion more often than just Sundays. I wasted time with God.

I had been doing pottery at a local college for more than six years and was just getting good at it when the Loma Prieta earthquake hit in October, 1989. I was in the pottery studio "throwing a pot" on the wheel. First I watched the building bend, then I headed for the door where everyone else was also going. Things were flying everywhere, and there was no shelter. Before I could get out the door, a tall, wide mirror crashed over my feet causing me to lose my balance. The floor moved one way, the door another, and I was shoved like a battering ram, head first, bent at the waist, into the metal door frame. I herniated seven discs and had C6 nerve damage in my right arm. After six months of severe pain and disability, I underwent a discectomy. After the surgery, I had limited use of my arm but still had chronic neck and arm pain. I got through the time with the Eternal Word Television Network daily. Mother Angelica and her programs re-taught me my Faith and a lot more I hadn't known. I couldn't go out much, but I had Mother Angelica, God, and through the telephone, my AA and church friends.

About ten months later, just as I was beginning to adjust and surrender to God's Holy will, I was rear-ended in an auto accident. Further injury to my neck caused nerve damage and pain in both legs and both arms. I could walk with a cane, but had muscle cramping and constant pain everywhere. Most of the damage and pain were in the right arm and left leg, but all four of my limbs were affected. Through it all, I continued with the Carmelites and was professed "until death" to live the Carmelite Rule in December, 1991. In January, 1992, I became the new Formation Directress of our little community.

At about this time, the priests at my church began to change things. The changes were so drastic and so contrary to the teachings of the Magisterium and the Holy Father that I had to leave and join another parish. It broke my heart to quit the choir and leave my friends, but I had to be true to my conscience.

The same thing was happening in my Carmelite community. As Formation Directress I was supposed to teach the new members of the community from a booklet that contained questionable ideas and meditation techniques from Eastern religious thought and New Age philosophy. I could not teach from that book and protested to my superiors and the community as a whole. The conflict that developed resulted in a split in the community which has caused me great grief. The community no longer meets, though I pray for restoration and a return to orthodoxy, I am now a lone Carmelite.

Meanwhile my physical condition had deteriorated. I had surgery again but I am now worse than before. I am on a walker which I can only use for short periods because I can't stand long nor can I lean with my arms. I hurt terribly in all four limbs. I burn all over and ache all the time. I am never without at least moderate pain. Some nights it is so severe I cannot sleep. I wear a large crucifix around my neck all the time, as it is a comfort to me. I am partaking with Christ in his Passion. I hold Jesus in my hands and kiss his head, hands, feet and side — his most Sacred Wounds — and I am comforted in my pain. I am closer than ever to him in my suffering than I ever would have been without it. Without this suffering I probably would have lost God and lost my soul.

If I had died before my conversion, I probably would have gone to hell. When I was with my ex-boyfriend, I was involved in New Age occultisms like astrology, TM, and astrological charts. He was heavily into Hinduism, Zen, and all the Eastern philosophies along with Thoreau, Madame Blavatsky and the theosophists, and the founders of New Age philosophy, which isn't new at all but as old as Satan himself. Once when I was sleeping at my ex-boyfriend's place alone, I woke to find an evil spirit hovering over me. I saw it and felt the evil and it scared me to death. When I screamed, it disappeared. I put on a scapular and a rosary and prayed to Our Lady, Saint Michael and my Guardian Angel to protect me. I was aware that this spirit wanted me. It had my ex-boyfriend, and it almost had me. I realized I wasn't playing around with toys or harmless things; these things were dangerous, and my immortal soul was at stake. I rejected the New Age and the occult and all that went with it. I don't know why the good Lord chose to give me the graces to "see" when others are clearly blinded.

I do know I am grateful to him. I am grateful for this gift of suffering because I am so close to him. I still take it one day at a time. I have a "maintenance program" now, as we say in AA. I work the steps daily — they are part of my life and I continue to be an involved, loyal, and practicing Roman Catholic on a daily basis. My prayer life is most important: it is food for my soul. Without it my soul would surely die. My God is personal and I love him in each of his persons. I love the Blessed Trinity. If I may borrow Father Ray Borque's prayer I heard on EWTN, which I say every night:

> Father, I adore You;
> Father, I love You;
> Father, please take care of me.
> Jesus, I adore You (in the Most Blessed Sacrament);
> Jesus, I love You (in the Most Blessed Sacrament);
> Jesus, please save me.
> (I add: Jesus I trust in You.)
> Holy Spirit, I adore You;
> Holy Spirit, I love You;
> Holy Spirit, please guide me.

I add:
> Holy Spirit, set me on fire with Your love;
> Holy Spirit, make me a true soldier in the Lord's Army.

Through this prayer I have a deep and personal love relationship with each person of the Blessed Trinity. My comfort lies in Jesus Crucified, in His Most Sacred Heart, His Most Sacred Body, His Most Precious Blood, His Most Holy Passion, His Most Blessed Mother Mary and Her Sorrowful and Immaculate Heart, and the three Divine Persons of the Most Blessed Trinity, Father, Son, and Holy Spirit. May God be praised for his goodness to me now and forever!

Paulette runs a hot line for others who need spiritual and emotional help with problems such as those she has described in this chapter. She is a secular Carmelite and a novice in a religious Order called the Handmaids of Nazareth.

Our Sunday Visitor...
Your Source for Discovering the Riches of the Catholic Faith

Our Sunday Visitor has an extensive line of materials for young children, teens, and adults. Our books, Bibles, booklets, CD-ROMs, audios, and videos are available in bookstores worldwide.

To receive a FREE full-line catalog or for more information, call **Our Sunday Visitor** at **1-800-348-2440**. Or write, **Our Sunday Visitor** / 200 Noll Plaza / Huntington, IN 46750.

Please send me: __ A catalog
Please send me materials on:
  __ Apologetics and catechetics   __ Reference works
  __ Prayer books   __ Heritage and the saints
  __ The family   __ The parish

Name_____
Address_____Apt._____
City_____State___Zip_____
Telephone ( )_____

                                                        A73BBABP

Please send a friend: __ A catalog
Please send a friend materials on:
  __ Apologetics and catechetics   __ Reference works
  __ Prayer books   __ Heritage and the saints
  __ The family   __ The parish

Name_____
Address_____Apt._____
City_____State___Zip_____
Telephone ( )_____

                                                         A73BBABP

Our Sunday Visitor
200 Noll Plaza
Huntington, IN 46750
1-800-348-2440
OSVSALES@AOL.COM

Your Source for Discovering the Riches of the Catholic Faith